ANDROID FOR TABLETS
WELCOME

Tablets have only been around for a few years, but they're all anyone talks about in technology today. And the most dynamic and fast-moving area of the tablet market today is Android tablets.

That's what this guide is all about: we've packed it with tips, in-depth guides and reviews to help you discover the world of Android tablets. Naturally, all the basics are covered, but there's much more to get your teeth into besides browsing the web and setting up email.

Android tablets are hugely flexible, expandable via apps – we review more than 60 – and even extra hardware. So we've made sure this guide includes all the information you need, illustrated with clear screenshots and step-by-step walkthroughs to help you get the most out of your tablet.

FIRST STEPS

We start at the very beginning, showing you how easy it is to set up an Android tablet from scratch, and introduce all the key features, focusing on Google's latest tablet software: Android 4.3, also known as Jelly Bean.

Every Android tablet comes with a set of core applications, from the web browser to the gallery and camera apps. We reveal how they work, and how to make best use of them.

IN DEPTH

There are also a wealth of apps that let you put your tablet to work as an office workhorse, use your tablet as a giant satnav, and even as a mobile gaming, music and movie-watching machine.

One of the biggest problems is the sheer number of apps to choose from, so each chapter includes our roundup of the key apps, whether office software or games. These include free options, so you may not need to spend a penny.

HARDWARE GUIDE

If you haven't bought your tablet yet, we have key choice covered. Our reviews gather together 13 models, from the most cost-effective to the lightest, fastest, sexiest hardware around. Whether your budget is £99 or £400, we'll make sure you make the right choice.

Our reviews don't pull any punches. Each tablet has been thoroughly assessed using a suite of challenging lab-based tests that reveal how fast it is, how long its battery lasts in real-world use and the quality of each screen.

In short, whether you're thinking of buying, have already bought an Android tablet or are simply curious to know more, this is the guide for you.

Jonathan Bray is *PC Pro*'s reviews editor and resident Android tablet expert

Jonathan Bray

Jonathan Bray

Editor
jonb@pcpro.co.uk

ANDROID FOR TABLETS
CONTENTS

CHAPTER 4
BEYOND THE BASICS
64

We uncover some of the more unusual tasks your Android tablet is capable of. Discover how to turn your tablet into a productivity tool to rival a laptop, an ebook reader and even a giant satnav.

CHAPTER 5
HARDWARE REVIEWS
86

If you haven't bought a tablet already, you'll find everything you need to make your choice in this chapter. We've reviewed 13 tablets that cover the full range of prices, from bargain basement to premium iPad rivals.

In this chapter

ANDROID FOR TABLETS
THE BASICS

If you've bought this guide then you're either about to buy a tablet or have just bought one. So what next? Over the next few pages, we reveal exactly what makes an Android tablet tick. You'll find out how to set one up from scratch, how to download and install your very first Android app, and why Android for tablets is so good and so different from the Apple iPad.

ANATOMY OF A TABLET

They may all look the same, but not all tablets are made equal. What separates one from another? And how do you go about choosing the best one for you? We reveal all

So what exactly is a tablet, and what differentiates one from another? It is, fundamentally, an LCD panel with a computer crammed behind it – a touchscreen laptop without a keyboard, if you will. So that display is the first thing you'll need to consider before deciding to buy.

Size is critical. If you're a bookworm and want a device mainly to read on, you should opt for a tablet with a 7in or 8in screen. Most 10in tablets are relatively heavy and uncomfortable to hold in one hand for long periods. A 7in tablet is easier to just sling in a bag.

A 10in screen really comes into its own for web browsing, entertainment and gaming. Web pages become easier to navigate and read, movies more compelling, and flicking through your photo collection on the sofa becomes a real pleasure.

The type of touchscreen you'll find on a tablet varies, too. The vast majority of modern tablets have a super-sensitive capacitive screen, which allows you to tap lightly, sweep gently, and scroll, pinch and drag with little effort.

Not all Android tablets are made equal, though. Most manufacturers use special coatings on the surface of a touchscreen to ensure your finger slides and slips across its surface; some, however, skimp on this coating, resulting in a screen that sticks under your finger. Screens without coatings are also more difficult to clean.

THE EXTRAS

Most tablets also have a camera, but do check what type before you buy. To save money, some only have a low-quality front-facing camera, intended mainly for video calls over the web. Others may not have a flash.

You'll need to check the amount of storage space, too. Most larger tablets come with at least 16GB of storage built in, which is big enough for a sizeable collection of apps, music, video and games. Some low-cost

A front-facing camera is useful for carrying out video calls to family overseas

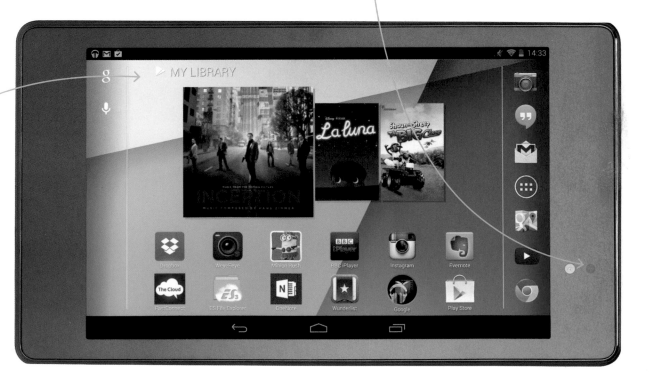

The screen is the most important part of any Android tablet

models, however, keep costs down by specifying 4GB or less.

The final big differentiating factor between one tablet and the next is connectivity; that is, how many ports and sockets it has. The most common is a USB connector – you use this to connect your tablet to a PC or Mac for general file transfer – but there are other options. Many come with HDMI outputs so you can connect your tablet directly to your HDTV. Some also allow you to connect USB memory sticks, while others – such as the Asus Transformers – come with a keyboard dock to convert tablet into laptop.

Many come with an expansion slot, allowing you to increase storage. This usually takes the form of a microSD slot, the same type of slot as you'll find in a smartphone. Occasionally, you'll find a tablet with a full-sized SD card slot, which allows you to use the type of memory card most cameras use.

NFC is becoming an increasingly common sight on modern mobile devices, and Android tablets are no exception. NFC allows you to transfer small files and contacts easily between two devices, and can be used to make Bluetooth pairing a simple matter of touching two devices together.

You don't get many buttons around the edges of most Android tablets because most controls are carried out using the touchscreen. On the Nexus 7, these are on the top-right edge of the tablet: a power button and volume control.

The quality of cameras on the rear of tablets is improving all the time. However, don't expect them to match the cameras in top-end smartphones.

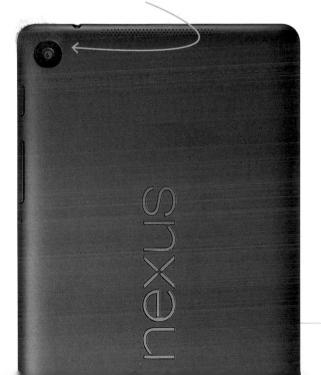

Watch out for tablets that don't have any form of memory expansion, which comes in the shape of a microSD slot. Tablets such as the Nexus 7 – pictured here – are fantastic devices, but if you run out of storage space the only way to remedy the situation is to delete files or uninstall apps.

With smaller Android devices such as the Nexus 7, you usually charge and transfer data using the tablet's USB connection, connected to a laptop or PC. Larger tablets, however, often require more power, and need plugging into the mains.

WHAT IS ANDROID?
You've probably heard a lot about it, but what's all the fuss about? Why should you buy an Android tablet instead of one from Apple? You'll find the answer to this question, and more, right here

Y ou'll probably be quite familiar with our friendly green man: the Google Android logo is liberally scattered across the windows of every major mobile phone emporium in the country. But what exactly is Android? And what makes it so different to Apple's offering?

In essence, Google Android is an operating system just like Microsoft Windows or Mac OS. And as with any laptop or desktop PC, an Android tablet will come with a version of the Android OS preinstalled.

An operating system is like a fancy control panel: it deals with the complicated stuff, talking to the computer's core hardware in a language it understands, while allowing you to push buttons and flick switches to get things done. Without an OS, you'd have to type complicated lines of code to get it to do even the simplest of things.

The difference between a standard computer OS and Android is that, where Windows and Mac OS were designed to be controlled via a keyboard and mouse, Android has been designed to be operated using a touchscreen. For instance, it uses finger-sized buttons and controls. It also supports "gestures", such as flick to scroll and the famous pinch-to-zoom gesture first implemented by Apple in the original iPhone.

THE SPICE OF LIFE
As with Windows, Android comes preinstalled on all manner of devices, from a wide range of manufacturers. You'll find Android on smartphones, compact tablets with 7in screens and larger tablets at 10in or above. Some manufacturers have even attempted, with limited success, to

Android tablets come in all different shapes and sizes. The Asus Transformer Pad, for instance, looks like any standard laptop, but it runs Android and can be converted from laptop to tablet simply by unhooking the screen from the keyboard base.

put Android on laptops and PCs. And most of the big names in the consumer electronics industry have built entertainment devices on Android: Samsung, Motorola, Acer and Asus to name but a few.

This means there's a huge variety of tablets with Android on board. Flick to Chapter 5 and you'll find reviews of powerful 10in tablets like the Asus Memo Pad FHD 10, smaller compact tablets such as Amazon's Kindle Fire HD 7 and Google's very own Android device, the Nexus 7. There's healthy competition among manufacturers of Android tablets, leading to greater choice for you.

THE ANDROID DIFFERENCE
As well as variety of choice, Android tablets hold other advantages over the Apple iPad and other manufacturers' tablets, too. One of these is connectivity. On an Apple device, there's no way of expanding the memory, for instance, but on most Android tablets you can usually slot in a card to boost the amount of storage space. Rather than being stuck with whatever you can afford when you buy, with most Android tablets you can add storage by up to 32GB when the need arises.

Another advantage of Android tablets is you can drag and drop whatever files you like in and out of the tablet's

TIP
Wondering which Android tablet to buy? We review all the best models later in this guide. See chapter 5.

Manipulate lists, web pages and photos using intuitive "gestures" instead of buttons and scrollbars.

memory. If you want to use software to synchronise your music, video and photos, you're not limited in your choice either as there are plenty of options.

Widgets, meanwhile, give you a window on all manner of your personal information directly from the tablet's homescreen, Apple's iPads can't offer this sort of rich interaction. And with these widgets offering at-a-glance updates, they can save a lot of time, too.

The biggest advantage with Android, though, brings us back to that variety of choice. If you buy into the Android way of doing things, your future upgrade options aren't dictated by the whims and mood of a single manufacturer. If you see a tablet in the shops made by a different manufacturer, you can simply make the switch and take all of your apps with you. And if you can't afford to

buy the top-end devices, there are plenty of budget Android tablets to choose from.

In short, Android is a much more flexible operating system than its main rival. It's available on more devices at more price points, it doesn't carry as many restrictions, and it leaves your future choices much more open.

THE APPLE ADVANTAGE

But we shouldn't be blind to Apple's advantages. It's the most established tablet, and Apple exerts a lot more control over things than Google does. Apple checks each and every new app before it's made available, which helps weed out substandard offerings of dubious value. The quality of its App Store is high, whereas Google Play can often seem like a bit of a Wild West.

By controlling the hardware as well, you can be confident of a slick interface and smooth performance with any iPad. The newer Android tablets made by big-brand companies all include fast processors and lots of memory, but there are dozens of Android tablets made by manufacturers that have poor build quality and weak specifications.

As such, be careful before you buy. If you're still on the lookout for a new tablet, read our reviews.

One of the major advantages of Android is that you can switch tablet manufacturer and still take the apps you've purchased with you.

Android
a potted history

Android started out life in 2008 on a smartphone. At the time, the only rivals to the Apple iPhone were complicated and fiddly to use on a touchscreen (such as Windows Mobile), or were corporate devices targeted specifically at business people and didn't support touch operation at all (such as the older BlackBerrys).

Google spotted a gap in the market and, in partnership with Taiwanese smartphone manufacturer HTC, produced the G1 smartphone. It was plagued with problems: battery life was poor, it was very basic and there weren't many apps to start with either.

Google quickly improved Android, however, moving from version 1 to 1.5, then 1.6. Since then, it's gone from strength to strength, moving through the gears with versions 2 to 2.3 before introducing Android 3, the first tablet-specific version. Since Android 4 arrived, there have been several major updates, all leading towards the very latest version, 4.4, due to arrive on select devices in late 2013.

Google gives each version of Android a dessert-related codename; the upcoming version is known as KitKat. Other notable codenames include Jelly Bean (version 4.1), Ice Cream Sandwich (version 4), Honeycomb (version 3), Gingerbread (version 2.3), and Cupcake (version 1.5).

TABLETS VS E-READERS

Colour e-readers such as the Amazon Kindle Fire appear to be capable of doing all that an Android tablet can. So which should you buy?

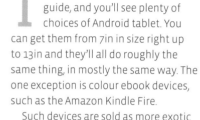

Take a look at the rear of this guide, and you'll see plenty of choices of Android tablet. You can get them from 7in in size right up to 13in and they'll all do roughly the same thing, in mostly the same way. The one exception is colour ebook devices, such as the Amazon Kindle Fire.

Such devices are sold as more exotic versions of their black-and-white e-reader cousins when, in fact, they're totally different. Under the skin, they have much more in common with a standard Android tablet. All of the Kindle Fire HD devices (and colour readers produced by other manufacturers such as Kobo and Barnes & Noble) use the Android operating system; they just dress it up differently (see opposite for what to expect from an Amazon device).

A Kindle Fire or Fire HD e-reader will therefore be capable of doing almost everything an Android tablet can. You can, of course, read your Amazon Kindle books on such a device, but it's also possible to play games, run apps, listen to music, and watch movies and TV programmes on them.

There are some advantages to buying an e-reader tablet instead of a plain Android device. They can be simpler to use, with a more logical user interface, and more convenient, too. When you buy a Kindle Fire, for example, it will arrive already linked to your Amazon account so you don't need to go through a setup procedure. You'll also see any ebooks you already own on other Kindles, and the same goes for any MP3 music bought through Amazon's MP3 service.

LOCK-IN

However, there are some disadvantages. to be aware of. Amazon wants you to use its own app store, so you won't be able to access any apps you've bought from Google Play on other devices. The same applies for ebooks and music.

Conversely, a standard Android tablet can do everything a specilised e-reader can. You can download the Kindle app for reading books, the Amazon Music App for listening to your Amazon MP3 files – you can even use the same movie-streaming service, Lovefilm, and the Amazon Appstore – plus any other download service you please.

Unless you really want convenience, then, it doesn't make much sense to buy a colour ebook reader, especially one from Amazon. You're far less restricted by a standard Android tablet.

Download the Kindle app to read books on your Android tablet.

WALKTHROUGH *The Kindle Fire interface*

Movie streaming comes from Lovefilm.

The Fire HD's interface is different to standard Android.

You can read your Amazon ebooks on a Fire, just like a standard Kindle.

The Amazon Appstore isn't as well stocked as Google Play

1
Amazon's Kindle Fire tablets are based on Android and do similar things, but look quite different. The first sign of this is the bold, main homescreen, which displays a scrollable list of recent items in the centre and suggested purchases below.

2
The user interface is split up into different sections, depending on content. Unsurprisingly, books is one of these. If you've ordered ebooks from Amazon before, you'll find these already setting in this section, ready to be downloaded, and you can buy more by quickly tapping Store.

3
Once downloaded, reading a book is much like using an ereader, but with a few more options available to you. It's possible to change the background colour, for instance, to a more eye-friendly sepia.

4
The advantage of owning a tablet is, of course, you can do other things, like watching video. The Kindle Fire has Lovefilm's movie streaming service built right in, which makes it child's play to browse and stream films.

5
The Music section is tied closely to Amazon's MP3 service. As with the Books section, any music you've already bought via Amazon will appear here, ready to download onto the tablet or stream directly from the web.

6
Just like any other Android tablet, the Kindle Fire range of tablets can be used to run games and apps. Apps are installed from the Amazon Appstore rather than Google Play, however, which has a much more limited choice.

7
One thing you get from the Amazon Appstore that you don't get from Google Play, however, is a free app every day. You don't have to download this, but it's a good way of building up a collection without spending any money.

FIRST STEPS

Before you can use your tablet to the fullest, you need to connect it to the internet and set it up with all your online accounts and services – think Gmail in particular. Here's a quick guide to the process

When you switch on your tablet for the very first time, there are a number of things you need to do before you can exploit its full potential.

First up is the job of connecting your new tablet to the internet: you'll need to be online before you can download and install new apps and games, and make use of the many entertainment services offered by Google and others.

Even if you've bought a 3G-enabled tablet, the easiest way to do this is via your home wireless connection, so make sure you know the name of your wireless network (often referred to as the SSID) and its password. If you're unsure about these details, you should find it tucked away in the settings of any computer or laptop that already connects to the wireless network. As a

last resort, contact the company that provides your internet connection.

Once you've provided all the information about your wireless network, you'll be asked for a Google username and password. It needs this to synchronise your email, calendar and contact information. Also, without a Google account, you won't be able to access Google Play to download and install apps on your tablet. We provide a walkthrough of the process opposite, and if you don't have a Google account your tablet will guide you through the setup process.

To purchase apps from Google Play, you'll also need to provide your credit card details. If you have an Android phone or have paid for Google services, you may have already done this and you can start shopping immediately.

FOR THE CHILDREN

Since Android 4.2, Google has thankfully catered for owners with a family who'll all want their turn with the tablet. The primary user can now set up multiple user accounts for adults, each of which is effectively isolated from the others – each user has their own Google accounts, email, settings, apps and credit card to use as they please.

That's not all. Android also supports restricted accounts for children, or for other users who you perhaps don't trust with your new tablet. You can control everything for these accounts, even going so far as disabling every feature except, say, the camera. The user won't be able to re-enable these features, nor access any of the tablet's files or settings. You have full control, which brings peace of mind.

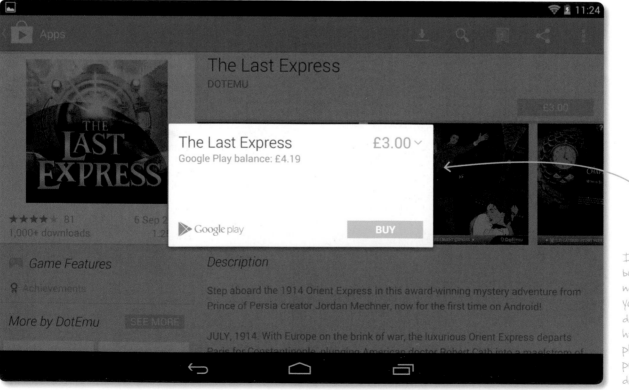

If you want to buy apps, you'll need to give your credit card details. If you have an Android phone, you've probably already done this.

1

The first thing you need to do is tell Google which region you're in. If your country isn't preselected, tap the menu and scroll through the list of countries, select it with a tap of your finger and then press the Next button.

2

Your tablet will now scan for available wireless networks, one of which should be yours. Once it's finished, you'll probably see a number of options. If you don't see your network in the list, you might be out of range (or it might not be switched on!). Move a little closer to your router and hit the Refresh button. Select your network by tapping it, then press the Next button to move on.

3

The keyboard will pop up at this point and you'll be asked to enter a password. This is the password you normally use to connect your laptop to your chosen wireless network. If no-one's looking over your shoulder, select the "Show password" option to make sure you don't make any mistakes on the onscreen keyboard. Tap Connect to proceed and wait for the next screen.

4

Google will then ask if it's okay to use your location to collect anonymous data and improve search results. If you don't want to reveal your location, untick the first one. If you untick the second option, your search results won't be "localised", which means if you search for "supermarkets", say, retail places near you won't appear at the top of search results. Tap Next.

Join Google+

Google+ makes sharing on the web more like real-life sharing.

⊙ **Circles**
The easiest way to share what matters most, online

📷 **Instant Upload**
Easily sync all of your photos from all your devices.

6

You only need a Google account; joining Google+ is optional.

Your name will be used to personalise much of the tablet experience.

Welcome
Deutsch
English (United Kingdom)
English (United States)
1

Select Wi-Fi
pcpro24g
Secured with WPA2 (WPS available)
pcpro5g
Secured with WPA2 (WPS available)
DPL
Secured with WPA2
2

This tablet belongs to...

The tablet uses your name to personalise some apps.

John

7

pcpro24g
pcpro5g
Signal strength   Excellent
Security   WPA2 PSK
3

Google services

Backup

✓ Use your Google Account to back up your apps, settings (such as bookmarks and Wi-Fi passwords) and other data.

✓ Bring apps, settings and other data to this tablet that you previously backed up to your Google Account.

4

Got Google?

Do you have a Google Account?

If you use Gmail or Google Apps, answer Yes.

5

5

If you already have a Google account from Gmail or another Android device, enter your username and password and hit "Sign in". If you don't have an account, create one here, as it will be your tablet hub from now on. If a message appears telling you there's been a problem, tap the Back button and enter the email address and password yourself on the following screen.

6

You can also join other Google services such as Google+, a social network that's a bit like Facebook, and is based around your Gmail contacts and account. If you're not interested, or just want to get the tablet set up, you can skip this step.

7

Finally, on the next screen, give the tablet your name if it doesn't come up automatically. This name will be used to greet you, and inserted into various apps and services to save you time and to make things more personal to you. That's it! Enjoy your new Android tablet.

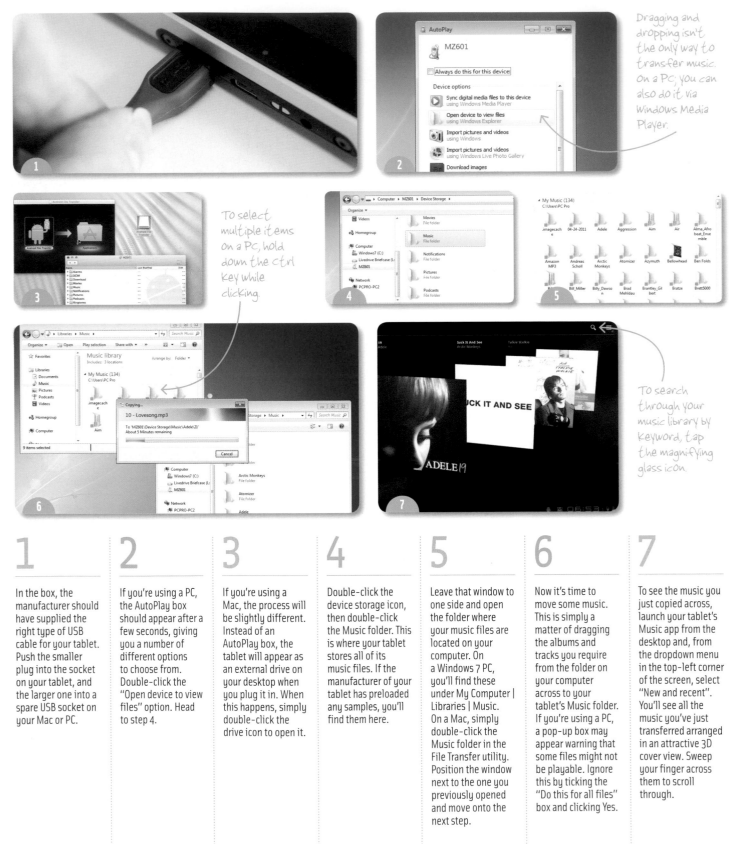
Dragging and dropping isn't the only way to transfer music. On a PC, you can also do it via Windows Media Player.

To select multiple items on a PC, hold down the ctrl key while clicking.

To search through your music library by keyword, tap the magnifying glass icon.

1

In the box, the manufacturer should have supplied the right type of USB cable for your tablet. Push the smaller plug into the socket on your tablet, and the larger one into a spare USB socket on your Mac or PC.

2

If you're using a PC, the AutoPlay box should appear after a few seconds, giving you a number of different options to choose from. Double-click the "Open device to view files" option. Head to step 4.

3

If you're using a Mac, the process will be slightly different. Instead of an AutoPlay box, the tablet will appear as an external drive on your desktop when you plug it in. When this happens, simply double-click the drive icon to open it.

4

Double-click the device storage icon, then double-click the Music folder. This is where your tablet stores all of its music files. If the manufacturer of your tablet has preloaded any samples, you'll find them here.

5

Leave that window to one side and open the folder where your music files are located on your computer. On a Windows 7 PC, you'll find these under My Computer | Libraries | Music. On a Mac, simply double-click the Music folder in the File Transfer utility. Position the window next to the one you previously opened and move onto the next step.

6

Now it's time to move some music. This is simply a matter of dragging the albums and tracks you require from the folder on your computer across to your tablet's Music folder. If you're using a PC, a pop-up box may appear warning that some files might not be playable. Ignore this by ticking the "Do this for all files" box and clicking Yes.

7

To see the music you just copied across, launch your tablet's Music app from the desktop and, from the dropdown menu in the top-left corner of the screen, select "New and recent". You'll see all the music you've just transferred arranged in an attractive 3D cover view. Sweep your finger across them to scroll through.

1

Since Android 4.2, users have been able to create multiple accounts, each with their own apps and settings, so you can safely hand your tablet to other family members without worrying about purchases on your credit card or nosy siblings rummaging through your emails. To set this up, drag down the top-right of the screen to access Settings, then scroll down and tap Users.

2

There are two types of account. You can create a straightforward new user, much like your own primary account but with its own credit card and Google logins. Or you can create a restricted account, which is ideal for children, as you can control which apps and settings they can access. We'll show you both, starting with a new User.

3

Follow the instructions to create your new User account, bearing in mind you'll need the person with you when you do. You'll be kicked back to the lockscreen, but this time with two user icons at the foot of the screen. Switch to the new user and unlock the tablet, then Android will take you through a similar setup procedure to your initial one. And that's it: two user accounts.

4

Setting up a restricted account is different, but its security settings apply to normal accounts, too, so it's worth reading even if you don't have any children.

With two types of user, you can easily add extra accounts for adults and children or even guests.

5

To restrict an account, you need to set up a lock method: face unlock, pattern, PIN or password. You can try each to see which you like best, and once you're done the new user won't be able to get into their account without you present to unlock the device.

6

You can control a huge range of settings for this account by enabling and disabling features in the restrictions list. You might want to enable the Games section of the Play Store, for example, but not the Chrome browser or Apps section. It's up to you.

7

Once you're done, you can switch between the accounts from the lockscreen, but your primary account (and any others for which you've added one) will now require you to perform the unlock method you chose in setup. And that's it. What you've learned here is vital in keeping a tablet usable by every member of the family without leading to arguments or worse.

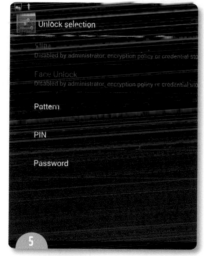

On a restricted account, you have full control over which apps and settings will be available.

All of your tablet's user accounts are on the lockscreen.

THE ANDROID 4 DESKTOP

Getting to know your tablet starts with the Android desktop. It's the heart of everything you do, from launching apps to checking your email, so it's well worth spending some time familiarising yourself with its features

Adding items to the desktop is as simple as opening the app drawer and dragging them out.

There are 101 different things you can do with your Android tablet, from browsing the web to playing videos, from streaming music to editing your holiday snaps, but it all starts at the Android desktop.

When you switch on your tablet it's the first thing you see; it's where you launch your favourite apps and games from, and you can use it to keep an eye on your email without lifting a finger.

If you're used to using a Windows PC, a laptop or a Mac, many features will look familiar. The main part of the screen, for instance, acts as a workspace you can customise and drop various items onto. These items can be shortcuts for apps you've downloaded, bookmarks for your favourite web pages or one of Android's interactive widgets – your Facebook feed, for instance, or the weather forecast.

Unlike a PC or Mac, though, Android isn't limited to only one desktop space. Sweeping your finger right or left on the desktop reveals more: Android 4 tablets offer up to five desktop spaces. Adding items to them is simply a matter of opening your Widgets list and dragging a widget out and onto one of those desktops. You'll see an outline appear showing where on the page it will sit before you drop it in place. You can also change you desktop background by holding a finger on any empty space.

SEARCH ME

But there's much more you can do from the desktop. At the top-left corner of the screen, you'll see the Google logo. This brings up the quick search window. From this one box, you can search the web, and the contents of your tablet all at once.

To use it, tap the Google logo and begin to type using the keyboard that pops up. Or hit the microphone icon beneath it and your tablet will try to recognise what you say. On the opposite side of the screen is the Apps icon (a circle with dots in). Tap this to bring up the so-called app drawer: a list of all the apps installed on your tablet.

At the very top of the screen is a thin black bar – the System Bar. In its right corner is a clock and status icons; drag down from here to change settings and get system information. And drag down from further left on the top bar to bring up alerts and notifications.

Finally, three further icons at the bottom of the screen are your main navigation controls: Back, Home and Recent Apps. Tapping the latter pops up a list of the apps you most recently used. Just tap one to launch it.

TIP

If your desktop doesn't look like the one pictured above, it's been customised. See p26 for more details.

Five desktops offer plenty of space to drag your shortcuts and widgets onto.

1

Tap the little circle with dots in on the right of your desktop to open the app drawer, then switch to the widgets menu from there. Anything in this list can be moved onto one of your desktops, and will update live. Just pick one you want, and tap and hold to drag it out to position it.

2

The press-and-hold technique can also be applied to app shortcuts and widgets to reposition or remove them. Hold a finger to the item you want to change and, after a second, a faint-blue grid appears. Keep your finger held to the surface then drag your item elsewhere. Remove it by dragging it to the cross icon that appears in the top-left corner, or move it to another desktop by dragging to the left or right.

3

The Analog Clock is just one of many widgets that comes preinstalled with Android 4. Not only does it look great, it also gives quick access to the alarm settings of your tablet – just tap it.

As you type, search results appear automatically here.

4

It's easy to search both the web and your tablet. Tap the Google icon on the homescreen to type using the onscreen keyboard. Results will appear as you type and they'll include both items on your tablet and results from the internet. You can select one of the options that appears onscreen as you type. If you prefer, tap the microphone and say your search term out loud.

5

Tapping the Recent Apps icon instantly brings up a list of the apps you've most recently used, complete with a thumbnail so you can see exactly where you left off. To relaunch any of the apps, tap its thumbnail.

6

Keep an eye on the top-left corner: this is where your latest email, calendar and download notifications appear. Tap the menu bar once to view messages in more detail, then tap an item to view it.

7

You can also access a number of quick settings from here: drag down from the top-right corner to adjust the screen brightness and switch into Aeroplane mode, which switches off all radios, such as Wi-Fi, GPS and 3G.

Notifications appear in the top-left corner.

THE KEYBOARD & SETTINGS

The keyboard isn't as basic as it looks. Take control of your Android tablet by learning the keyboard's hidden features and familiarising yourself with its hidden settings secrets

There's more to Android tablets than just the desktop. To use your tablet to the full, you'll need to familiarise yourself with other key elements. Take the keyboard: it's probably the part of Android you'll use the most after the desktop, but you need to explore its settings and practise using it before your typing gets fully up to speed.

Armed with a little knowledge, you'll be able to insert special symbols in a trice. Common symbols can be inserted with a simple long press: just look for keys that have secondary characters displayed in the top-right corner. And if the symbol you're looking for isn't there, or it's numbers you want, a quick tap of the "?123 key" will bring up more.

There's even a voice-recognition button lurking near the bottom-left corner, which is perfect for those long, fiddly spellings you're not quite sure of. But the key to quick, accurate typing with the Android 4 keyboard is to use Auto Correction and Show Correction.

The first corrects misspellings and typos every time you hit the spacebar or enter a punctuation mark, and it's so good you can let your fingers fly across the key-tops without worrying too much about hitting the right letter. Most of the time the keyboard will choose the right word for you.

As you practise your typing, keep an eye on the line just above the top row of keys. Here, Android displays the words it thinks you're typing based on the letters you've hit so far. Tap a word to insert it, then move to the next one.

You'll need to turn each of these options up to the maximum. Set Auto Correction to "Aggressive" and Show Correction suggestions to "Always show" in the keyboard settings (see overview, right) to reap the full benefit.

JOINED-UP WRITING

One relatively recent addition to the Android keyboard is gesture typing. Instead of tapping each letter individually to spell a word, you can simply swipe from letter to letter without releasing your finger. A blue line will briefly show your route around the keyboard, and the clever software will work out what word you're trying to spell, even if you're rather loose and shaky with your swiping. There are plenty more features to play with as well, so be sure to explore the Settings screen. We walk through some key options opposite.

> ## TIP
> Keep an eye on the narrow black strip just above the keyboard for word suggestions and spelling corrections.

Android's keyboard might look basic, but it harbours hidden depths; master these and you'll be typing almost as quickly as you can on a laptop keyboard.

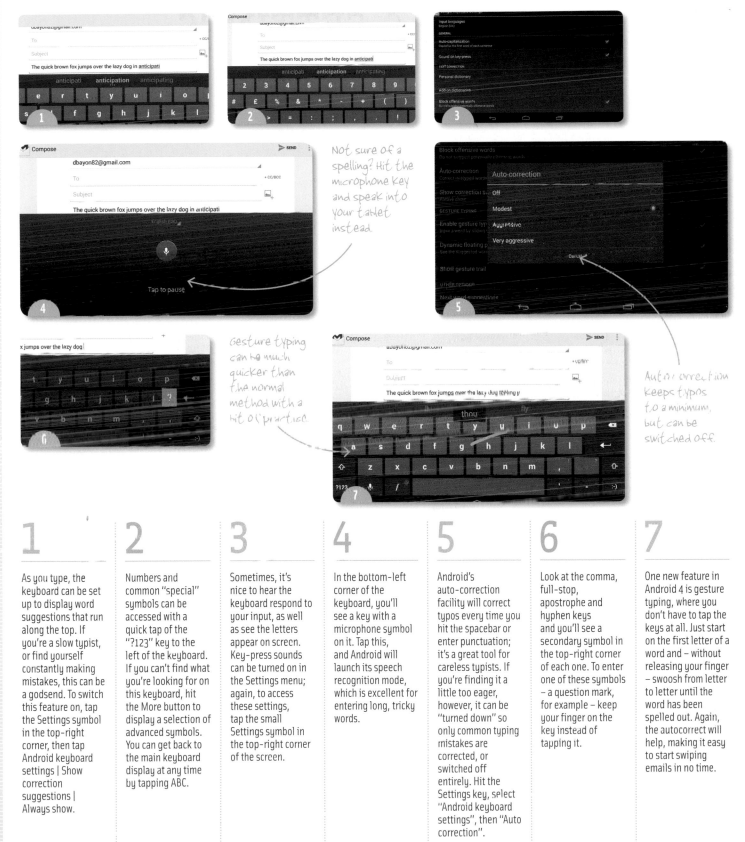

Not sure of a spelling? Hit the microphone key and speak into your tablet instead.

Gesture typing can be much quicker than the normal method with a bit of practice.

Auto-correction keeps typos to a minimum, but can be switched off.

1

As you type, the keyboard can be set up to display word suggestions that run along the top. If you're a slow typist, or find yourself constantly making mistakes, this can be a godsend. To switch this feature on, tap the Settings symbol in the top-right corner, then tap Android keyboard settings | Show correction suggestions | Always show.

2

Numbers and common "special" symbols can be accessed with a quick tap of the "?123" key to the left of the keyboard. If you can't find what you're looking for on this keyboard, hit the More button to display a selection of advanced symbols. You can get back to the main keyboard display at any time by tapping ABC.

3

Sometimes, it's nice to hear the keyboard respond to your input, as well as see the letters appear on screen. Key-press sounds can be turned on in the Settings menu; again, to access these settings, tap the small Settings symbol in the top-right corner of the screen.

4

In the bottom-left corner of the keyboard, you'll see a key with a microphone symbol on it. Tap this, and Android will launch its speech recognition mode, which is excellent for entering long, tricky words.

5

Android's auto-correction facility will correct typos every time you hit the spacebar or enter punctuation; it's a great tool for careless typists. If you're finding it a little too eager, however, it can be "turned down" so only common typing mistakes are corrected, or switched off entirely. Hit the Settings key, select "Android keyboard settings", then "Auto correction".

6

Look at the comma, full-stop, apostrophe and hyphen keys and you'll see a secondary symbol in the top-right corner of each one. To enter one of these symbols – a question mark, for example – keep your finger on the key instead of tapping it.

7

One new feature in Android 4 is gesture typing, where you don't have to tap the keys at all. Just start on the first letter of a word and – without releasing your finger – swoosh from letter to letter until the word has been spelled out. Again, the autocorrect will help, making it easy to start swiping emails in no time.

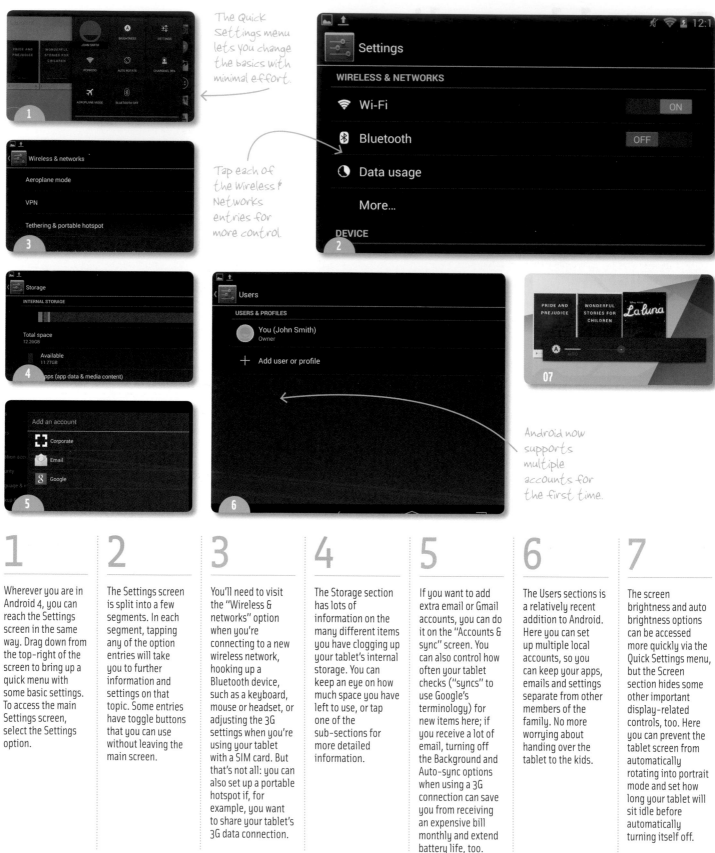

The Quick settings menu lets you change the basics with minimal effort.

Tap each of the Wireless & Networks entries for more control.

Android now supports multiple accounts for the first time.

1

Wherever you are in Android 4, you can reach the Settings screen in the same way. Drag down from the top-right of the screen to bring up a quick menu with some basic settings. To access the main Settings screen, select the Settings option.

2

The Settings screen is split into a few segments. In each segment, tapping any of the option entries will take you to further information and settings on that topic. Some entries have toggle buttons that you can use without leaving the main screen.

3

You'll need to visit the "Wireless & networks" option when you're connecting to a new wireless network, hooking up a Bluetooth device, such as a keyboard, mouse or headset, or adjusting the 3G settings when you're using your tablet with a SIM card. But that's not all: you can also set up a portable hotspot if, for example, you want to share your tablet's 3G data connection.

4

The Storage section has lots of information on the many different items you have clogging up your tablet's internal storage. You can keep an eye on how much space you have left to use, or tap one of the sub-sections for more detailed information.

5

If you want to add extra email or Gmail accounts, you can do it on the "Accounts & sync" screen. You can also control how often your tablet checks ("syncs" to use Google's terminology) for new items here; if you receive a lot of email, turning off the Background and Auto-sync options when using a 3G connection can save you from receiving an expensive bill monthly and extend battery life, too.

6

The Users sections is a relatively recent addition to Android. Here you can set up multiple local accounts, so you can keep your apps, emails and settings separate from other members of the family. No more worrying about handing over the tablet to the kids.

7

The screen brightness and auto brightness options can be accessed more quickly via the Quick Settings menu, but the Screen section hides some other important display-related controls, too. Here you can prevent the tablet screen from automatically rotating into portrait mode and set how long your tablet will sit idle before automatically turning itself off.

Portable audio

Tablet speakers will do a job, but if you want to fill a room you'll need something more powerful. Try these four portable audio solutions for size

Braven 650 Portable Wireless Speaker
Price: £160 Supplier: www.braven.eu

The Braven 650 isn't only gorgeous to look at, it's also sturdy enough to cope with the physical side of travel. Despite weighing a mere 340g, it contains a rechargeable battery that should last 12 hours at medium volume. Sound quality is impressive for a speaker of this size: while the bass won't blow your socks off, higher frequencies are well detailed.

Music Angel Friendz Portable Speaker
Price: £20 Supplier: www.mobile-fun.co.uk

This battery-powered speaker will connect to your tablet's headphone socket and boost the audio out into the room. It comes in many colours, and you can daisy-chain multiple speakers to boost the volume. Given the tiny size and low price, don't expect great sound quality, but it's perfectly good for keeping you entertained in a hotel room.

Native Union Switch
Price: £120 Supplier: www.nativeunion.com

The Switch is the Swiss Army knife of Bluetooth speakers. It contains three speaker drivers and a duplex microphone, so it can also be a speakerphone. Under a panel on the side there's a micro-USB port for charging the speaker, and a full-sized port for passing that power onto another device. Sound quality is pretty good for the size, too.

Pure Jongo S3
Price: £170 Supplier: www.johnlewis.com

This distinctive-looking portable speaker is actually meant as part of a Pure multiroom setup – you can use the Pure Android app to play your tracks. It works fine on its own, though, and with four speakers inside this little device the sound quality is good, complete with different audio profiles to suit the environment.

USING GOOGLE NOW

Branded as an "intelligent personal assistant", Google Now is one of your tablet's most smartest features. We show you how to set it up and how to make the most of it

TIP
If you're worried about privacy, you can turn off email linking or web history analysis in the settings.

Imagine having your very own secretary, always on hand to tell you when you have meetings coming up, check if your flight's on time, or warn you if there's a problem on your regular commute. All without any intervention or work on your part.

That's exactly what Google Now, one of Android's hidden gems, aims to do for you. Google Now appears whenever you tap the search box on the main home page of your Android tablet, and presents useful information – like those upcoming meetings and flights – in a series of "cards" below the search box.

It can also tell you about upcoming sports events and recent results, provide package tracking information and restaurant reservations. It knows when you're travelling, and will suggest places to visit based on where you are.

When you're in a different time zone, it will even automatically display the time at home and show a currency conversion box so you can quickly work out how much you're spending.

HOW IT WORKS

Google Now works its magic by analysing your search history, the contents of your emails and Google calendar, and by tracking your location via Wi-Fi and GPS. In order to make the most of it, it needs to be set up correctly.

Fortunately, this is simple and only a one-time job; just follow the onscreen instructions the first time you fire it up. Once this is done, you can sit back, relax and let Google Now take the reins.

Presenting handy facts isn't the only thing Google Now is good at, however.

You can also tell it to do things for you, such as set reminders, or ask it questions about the weather at a travel destination, for example.

Simply tap the microphone icon at the right of the search box at the top of the Google Now screen and say what you want to do – for example, "remind me to pay the milkman" – and Google Now will set up that reminder for you automatically.

And don't forget that Google Now is also a powerful search tool, able to simultaneously hunt through contacts, emails and other data stored on your tablet, as well as search the web using Google's fantastically powerful search engine. You can carry out a search using Google Now, just as you would on the Google website, by typing terms into the box at the top.

Google Now analyses your search history, email content, and your Google calender to present you with useful info when you tap the search box on your tablet's homescreen.

You can set up sports cards manually to keep you up to date on the teams you follow.

To get rid of sample cards, simply swipe them off the screen.

1

You can fire up Google Now in one of two ways: by tapping the search box at the very top of the main homescreen, or by holding a finger or thumb on the home icon at the centre of the bar at the bottom and dragging slowly upwards.

2

The first time you launch Google Now, you'll need to run through the setup process. There isn't much to this – just a series of screens, explaining what Google Now is for. Keep tapping Next until the Get Google Now! Screen appears, and then tap "Yes, I'm in" to finish.

3

You'll end up with a screen that looks something like this, with a search box at the top and a series of boxes below. In Google Now, these boxes are called "cards" and they present snippets of contextual information based on the time of day, your location, search history and the content of your Gmail inbox.

4

The first few of these cards are samples and suggestions, which you'll need to get rid of. To do this, simply swipe them off the screen to the left or right. Leave the Weather card on the screen, and tap the "Show more cards..." option at the bottom of the screen.

5

At this point, a series of cards, including info on upcoming birthdays and flight departures may appear. However, don't be surprised if no further cards appear. You may need to add some information manually first. To do that, tap the three dots in the bottom-right corner, then select Sample Cards to see a list of options and settings.

6

Most of the card types are automatic, but others, such as the Sports card, can be set up manually. Select the Settings option below the Sports heading and, on the following screen, tap Add team. Type the name of the team or teams you want to appear on your Google Now screen, then use the tablet's Back button to return to the main Google Now screen.

7

Your Google Now homescreen should now look a bit more busy, but it takes time for the service to really come into its own. Once you've started to carry around your tablet and used the calendar app a few times, more cards and useful information will begin to appear.

DIFFERENT ANDROID FLAVOURS

Even tablets running the same version of Android can look very different. Here we look at some of the software you might find on your tablet

The Samsung Galaxy Note comes with a stylus, and its Android feels very different...

TIP
Read the reviews in Chapter 5 to find out what manufacturers have done to the plain Android interface.

Jelly Bean, or Android 4.3, is the most recent version of Android to be released, and it's come a long way since the days of tablets having to use awkwardly magnified smartphone apps. Today's Android tablets are flexible and easy to use, so anyone can pick up one and get going in no time.

But what's all that software on your tablet, and why doesn't it look like the clean screenshots in this book? It's an important question, and there are two possible answers.

The first is that your tablet may run an older version of Android. As long as it's not too ancient, some of the settings and buttons may be in different places, and menus might have a different order and layout, but with the exception of the latest brand-new features, most of the things we show in this book should still be there somewhere.

The other answer is customisation. Tablet manufacturers are commercial companies and they want to make sure

you use more than just their hardware, which is why you'll often find a whole new interface "skin" laid over the top of normal Android. HTC has its Sense interface, Samsung has TouchWiz and there are several others. If you want to see the vanilla Android look, Google's own Nexus 7 shows just how stark the difference can be.

WHAT'S IN A SKIN?

But a third-party skin isn't necessarily something to be afraid of. They can be great to look at and use, and some of the applications preinstalled by manufacturers are genuinely useful, be it online music services or cloud storage, or even just customised camera and social apps. And often you'll find those menus don't just have a different layout; they've actually been enhanced with additional options, so play around to find out.

For tablets with an unusual screen size, extra apps can be vital – think

handwriting tools on a tablet with a bundled stylus, for example. It's always worth trying them out and, if you don't like any of them, some manufacturers will let you remove them to free up disk space.

A more recent trend involves content. Companies that also have their own content stores have begun to use tablets as a way to increase their customer base. Google opted to put books, videos and music right on the desktop with its Nexus 7, to tempt you into browsing and shopping for more. And Amazon takes the idea to the extreme, basing the entire interface of its Kindle Fire HD devices around recommendations of content from the Amazon store. You even have to pay extra to get a version that won't pester you with regular adverts. It can be annoying if you've bought expecting something a bit less intrusive, but if you like your content this approach can prove useful.

WALKTHROUGH *What you might find on your tablet*

Some, like this Asus tablet, will feature quick menus and customised app drawers.

A tablet that comes with a bundled stylus will usually have handwriting software preinstalled.

Always take the time to browse any included app stores, even if only to make sure you're not missing much

---

1

The Android basics are often tweaked first, so you might find your menus look different to the screenshots in this book. On this Samsung tablet, the settings and notifications area rises from the bottom-right of the screen and includes some extra options to play with.

2

A tablet with a bundled stylus will come with handwriting software, and a good one will build it into everything you do. Samsung lets you scrawl your way through emails, documents and even Google searches, so you can get used to keeping the pen in your hand at all times.

3

Some tablets customise the experience with their own recent apps lists or quick-launch bars. This Asus tablet comes with some commonly used core applications ready to open in a bar that pops up at the foot of the screen.

4

The standard Google app drawer isn't the most flexible feature, so manufacturers may tweak it to be more welcoming. Here, Asus has added a dropdown option to sort the apps into orders other than alphabetical.

5

If a tablet has a unique feature, expect to find a preinstalled app in place to make full use of it. Sony's Xperia Tablet Z has an IR transmitter for controlling TVs and other entertainment devices, and the excellent bundled remote-control app takes full advantage.

6

Your keyboard will often differ in layout and style compared to the standard keyboard in Android 4.3, but don't be alarmed. The labelling may differ slightly, but all the keys will be in there somewhere, and you'll very quickly get your typing up to speed.

7

Finally, everyone wants a slice of the money being spent on apps these days, so don't be surprised to find that your tablet manufacturer has installed its own stores. This example from Sony shows what you can expect: in some cases, there might be some useful tools on offer, but you always have the Google Play Store if these third-party stores are not to your liking.

HOW TO INSTALL APPS

Now you know your way around the Android OS, it's time to install a few apps. These are the difference between your tablet being a glorified touchscreen and the most useful piece of kit in your house

TIP

Look at our favourite entertainment apps on p42, games from p46, and our top business picks on p62.

While apps gained popularity through Apple's iPhone and Google Android phones, the larger screen space of a tablet gives them a new lease of life.

You can download an app to read novels on, interactive apps for your favourite magazines, apps for making free phone calls, apps for sharing files, shopping and more. In short, you can find an app to do pretty much anything you can think of, and the best thing about them is they're a doddle to install.

Your route for adding apps is the Google Play store, and you'll usually find a shortcut to it from your tablet's main desktop. There's a staggering amount of content waiting for you in the store, so it's helpfully split into six sections: Apps, Games, Movies & TV, Music, Books and Magazines. Google

will make recommendations on the homepage based on your previous downloads, and you'll find regular sales and special offers.

To get a feel for the sort of apps available for your tablet, choose the Apps section and click Categories from the menu at the top. If you have an app in mind, or a particular job you want an app to do, tap the magnifying glass icon in the bar at the top of the screen and use the onscreen keyboard to search the store by keyword.

INSTALLING APPS

Installing a free app is simple: just tap it to bring up the details page. This lets you view a description of the app, plus screenshots and user ratings. If you're happy, hit the green button and tap OK to agree to any terms and conditions.

The view will change to show the status of the download, before giving you an Open button to easily launch the app – you don't even have to leave the page.

Installing paid-for apps is almost as easy, and the Install button will clearly display the price to avoid any nasty surprises. Once you've entered your credit card details for the first app you buy, they're stored for later purchases. And if you don't like an app you've paid for, Google gives you a 15-minute grace period during which you can remove it for a full refund.

When you've installed an app, it will be added to your app drawer and appear on your homescreen. You're then free to drag it to another location. It pays to keep your apps organised from the beginning, as you'll quickly build up a large number of them.

The Google Play store is divided into sections, so you can easily browse for apps separately to music and other entertainment.

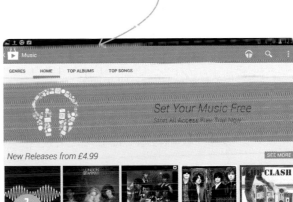

Google's increasingly impressive music options are explained in more detail in chapter 2.

Free apps can be downloaded without handing over any credit card details.

The Play Store isn't only about apps. It also has plenty of HD movies to choose from, complete with trailers to help you decide.

1

The Google Play Store is divided neatly into multiple sections so you can find the content you're looking for very easily. Choose from Apps, Games, Movies & TV, Music, Books and Magazines to see the best of those content types, or scroll down to see more recommendations curated by Google.

2

To get a better idea of the kind of apps that are available in the store, choose the Apps section and tap Categories in the top-left of the screen. The other section headings along the top are pretty self-explanatory and well worth exploring. In the Top Free section, you'll inevitably find Angry Birds somewhere near the top of the list, so let's install that as our first app.

3

The app page has lots of screenshots and plenty of information to help you decide whether you want to install or buy an app. Down the left, you'll find user ratings, the number of downloads, and the size and release date of the latest version. As this is a free app, the button on the right just says Install. Tap that now.

4

If this was a paid app, you'd have to deal with payment now, but for a free app the next stage will see a permissions box pop up. This might look daunting, but it's simply a heads-up to warn you which resources the app will use when you fire it up. It's nothing much to worry about, so go ahead and click OK.

5

Without leaving the app page, the info bar at the top will change to a download meter and then an install progress bar to indicate that your app is on its way. When it's done, it will appear on your homescreen, but you can also open the app from right there in the Play Store.

6

It's not only apps in the Google Play Store. There's a wide range of movies available in both standard and high definition. You can watch trailers before you choose and read all about the films. Watch your data usage, though, as video can really drain any monthly data allowances you may have.

7

And then there's music. Google is going big into the world of music, as you'll find out in Chapter 2. It's Google Play Music service lets you store your tracks safely on Google's servers, ready to be accessed from any device with an internet connection.

THE BASICS

FIRST APPS *to get you started*

You've got your new tablet and you're eager to get going, but which apps should you look to first? Try these ten must-haves before anything else

Dropbox
Price: **Free**

Your Android tablet already comes with Google Drive installed, but there's no doubt which is the most flexible, cross-platform file-syncing app out there: Dropbox. With a decent amount of free storage space, the ability to sync files across PC, Mac and all phones and tablets, and a range of paid-for accounts that make it a viable sharing tool for business, it's a must-have app for any serious technology lover. Plus, if you know someone who already uses Dropbox, ask them for a referral code and you'll both get some bonus storage space.

Facebook
Price: **Free**

You can fight the urge as much as you want, but eventually you'll be checking and updating Facebook on your tablet all day like the rest of us. To be fair, the official Facebook app has improved a lot from its early versions, which were a bit sluggish to use. It's now a fast and slick way to keep in touch with your friends and tell the world about your latest activities, and it has a big advantage over Google+, which is that everyone is already using it. There's also a Facebook Messenger app.

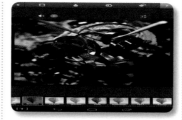

Twitter
Price: **Free**

With Twitter, you can talk to far more people than just your Facebook friends, and they can decide whether they want to follow your communications or not, so make sure you're interesting! The official app may not be to every Twitter user's tastes, but it's the easiest way to get going with the social network as a newbie. Once you're a bit of a Twitter pro, you can start thinking about using one of the more complex and powerful client apps in Chapter 3.

Instagram
Price: **Free**

If you're not already using it, Instagram is the social app based around your photos. It's also the app that gave the world those millions of arty personal shots with sepia tints and other quickly annoying image filters. Like it or hate it, playing around with your photos afterwards is part of the fun of Instagram, and it's become part of the mobile furniture. It's even integrated into many other social networks to make it as easy as possible to share your snaps.

Evernote
Price: **Free**

Evernote has been around for ages, but it's still hard to conclude that there's anything better than its simple yet powerful mix of note-taking, reminders, to-do lists and recordings, all of which are synced across pretty much any device and platform imaginable – both mobile and desktop. The number of services it's incorporated and tied in with has grown with each new release, so it's reaching the point where it renders many other popular apps redundant.

BBC iPlayer

Price: **Free**

Catch up on all the recent TV you've missed with the official BBC iPlayer app for Android. Programmes are available to watch in standard or high quality, with both live TV and recent popular showings to browse through. And the Android app also now includes downloads, which you can keep for up to 30 days and continue watching within seven days of the first play. We could also have included the similar catch-up apps from ITV and Channel 4 on this list, but it's hard to argue with the consistent quality of output from the BBC.

TuneIn Radio
Price: **Free**

One of the most popular free apps on the Play Store at all times, TuneIn Radio has all the features you'd expect: hundreds of radio stations divided up by region, and many more categorised into dozens of genres. As on the website, sports and news stations are given their own sections, and it's also possible to filter the thousands of stations by language. TuneIn supports podcasts as well, with shows organised into similar genres. For radio fans, this app is a must.

Sky+
Price: **Free**

If you're a Sky subscriber, this is a no-brainer. The Sky+ app isn't just a TV guide, it's a full remote control for your Sky box. It has interactive channel listings, complete with favourites, showing full programme information and Sky's highlights, and when you click Watch your TV responds instantly. Then you can flip to the live gesture interface and rewind what you're watching with a simple swipe. It's worth having just for the ability to set a recording while you're out.

QuickOffice
Price: **Free**

Google now owns this Android office suite, but it doesn't yet come preinstalled. You can create and edit Microsoft Word, Excel and PowerPoint files, and view PDF files, and it all links in seamlessly to your Google Drive cloud storage, so you can keep all your documents neatly filed in one place. As a bonus, you get extra Drive storage for linking QuickOffice, so it's worth downloading just for that. It's free now, but there's no guarantee it will be forever.

Amazon Kindle
Price: **Free**

Even if you don't choose to buy a Kindle Fire HD tablet, you can still install the free Kindle app on any other Android device and get access to every ebook you've ever bought from Amazon. The quality of the reading experience will depend on your tablet's screen, but the app can show colour images and supports easy jumping around between chapters and sections. It will sync your current page with your other Kindle devices, and there are loads of free books to try.

In this chapter

ANDROID FOR TABLETS
ENTERTAINMENT & GAMING

We've covered the basics: now it's time to get motoring. In this chapter, we revel in the sheer fun you can have with your Android tablet, from streaming TV and movies and accessing music on the move to reading magazines and snapping with your camera. And there's also the small matter of playing games...

SHOOTING A SCENE
While we'd never suggest replacing your DSLR with a tablet, many devices include decent cameras. Here's how to make the most of them, from capturing special moments to building panoramas

Tap the camera icon to change between photos and videos, or to access the panorama and photo sphere modes.

Most tablets include a camera, so you can snap stills and even use it like a camcorder. The process is straightforward: launch your tablet's Camera app and hit the Shutter button. There's normally a shortcut on the desktop, but, if not, launch the app drawer and select the Camera app from there.

You can leave it at that, shooting in automatic mode to your tablet's memory and browsing the results using the Gallery app. But by acquainting yourself with the Camera app's expert functions you'll shoot much better photos and video clips.

In Android 4.3, the various settings are found next to the Shutter button. Tap the settings icon above or to the right of the shutter (depending on how you're holding the tablet) to bring up all sorts of options, from flipping between the front and rear cameras to changing the look of your snaps.

If the colours look odd indoors – a little too blue or yellow – it's usually because the camera has set the white balance wrong. This can be fixed by adjusting the settings under the thermometer symbol. If you're uncomfortable tweaking the settings manually, but want to improve your photos, try one of the Scene modes. These include presets for action photography, beach snaps, sunsets and landscapes to help you get the best results possible.

Other options available here include setting a countdown timer for your next shot, toggling whether snaps retain location data from your tablet GPS, and even changing the resolution of the images being taken, which is useful if you're running low on storage space.

THE FUN SIDE
On the other side of the Shutter button is a camera icon, and this is where the fun starts. Tap that to change between photos and videos, and two other new modes: panorama and photo sphere.

With panorama mode, you can start at one end of a scene, begin capturing, then scan your camera across the rest of the scene. The tablet will do the hard work of taking the row of images and compiling them into one wide panoramic image.

The other option is even crazier. With a photo sphere, you begin by snapping a photo in the middle of what you want to capture, then use the anchor dots to capture further images around it. The software wraps them all together, so that with a bit of patience you can create a full 3D view of your location. The walkthrough shows it in action.

TIP
To take a self portrait, use the front-facing camera by tapping the rotate camera icon in the app's Settings menu.

1

In the Camera app, tap the camera icon next to the Shutter button to pull up the different modes. From left to right, they are: photo sphere, panorama, video capture, photo capture. First, we'll try the panorama mode.

2

You'll notice the capture window for a panorama is much smaller than normal. Point the tablet's camera to the left or right end of the scene you want to capture and be sure to frame it nicely in that box. Then press the Shutter button and slowly pan across the scene. If you go too fast, the app will flash red.

3

As you pan, the bar at the bottom of the screen will slowly fill up. When it's full, your panorama is taken, so try to align the end of the scene with that moment if you can. Then the app will process the panorama, taking all the shots it has from that pan and compiling them into one long image.

4

If you can't find the image, go to the Gallery app and choose the Camera folder. If you've followed the process correctly, you should see a long, thin image of your scene. If it doesn't look right, delete it and try again, perhaps moving more slowly for a clearer picture.

5

For a photo sphere, go back to the Camera app and tap the Modes button again, and choose the bubble-shaped photo icon. Here, the goal is to pick the centre spot of a scene, and then fill more and more photos around it. Hold up the camera and align the first shot, then keep moving to the edges of the image and aligning the dot to add more parts.

6

When you're done, just tap the shutter button again to stop capturing your photo sphere. Again, go to the Gallery app and choose the Camera folder, and you'll get your first glimpse of the results: a strange fish-bowl-style view of your scene. If it doesn't look right, try it again.

7

There's a lot more to experiment with, not least the photo and video modes of the camera. Tap the settings icon and try out all the different white balances and scene modes. You'll be taking great shots in no time.

A photo sphere can give a surreal fish-eye look to any scene.

ENTERTAINMENT & GAMING

WATCHING VIDEO

Enjoy the big screen on the small screen thanks to streaming and local video playback. We reveal exactly how to take advantage of on-demand services from the big broadcasters and how to convert your own videos for playback

One of the best things about a tablet is its large screen, in comparison to a smartphone, at least. It's great for all sorts of things, not least watching TV, movies or your own home-grown movie clips. And there are all sorts of ways you can do this with your Android tablet.

The easiest and simplest is via a streaming service. The YouTube app comes preinstalled on your tablet and gives you access to millions of clips, from funny snippets to movie trailers, and even full TV shows.

You'll find the YouTube app in your tablet's app drawer. If you're in the UK, we recommend you take advantage of the BBC iPlayer app in the Android Market, because it gives a smoother viewing experience than watching clips directly on the BBC website.

Another way to watch films and TV shows on your tablet is to stream them from your computer or a network-connected hard disk. There's a wide array of software on offer to do this, but Plex is the best we've seen. It costs around £3 from the Android Market and, after installing it on your laptop or PC, you'll be able to view all the video you have stored directly over your home network. It even works for music.

VIDEO RENTALS & DOWNLOADS

While streaming video is great, there are times when you won't have a fast enough internet connection or any at all. Instead, take advantage of your tablet's built-in video player and make sure you have a selection of video files stored in the tablet's memory.

Some tablets, such as Samsung's Galaxy Tabs, have their own video stores, where you can rent or buy videos to download and watch on your tablet's built-in video player. Google Play also offers a huge range of TV shows and films to stream and download, and there's a variety of other services you can try. Netflix and Lovefilm, for instance, offer subscription services that deliver unlimited access to their film and TV libraries.

For playing other files (whether downloaded or shot on your camcorder), it's a little more complicated. Android's built-in video player is fussy about what type of video files it will play, so copying files across to the tablet's memory can be hit and miss. You'll normally have to convert files first using an application on your PC.

> **TIP**
> Third-party video apps support more file types and have more options than the stock app. It's well worth downloading one.

You can watch BBC iPlayer programmes straight from the website, but the BBC iPlayer app is much easier to use and far more pleasant to browse programmes on.

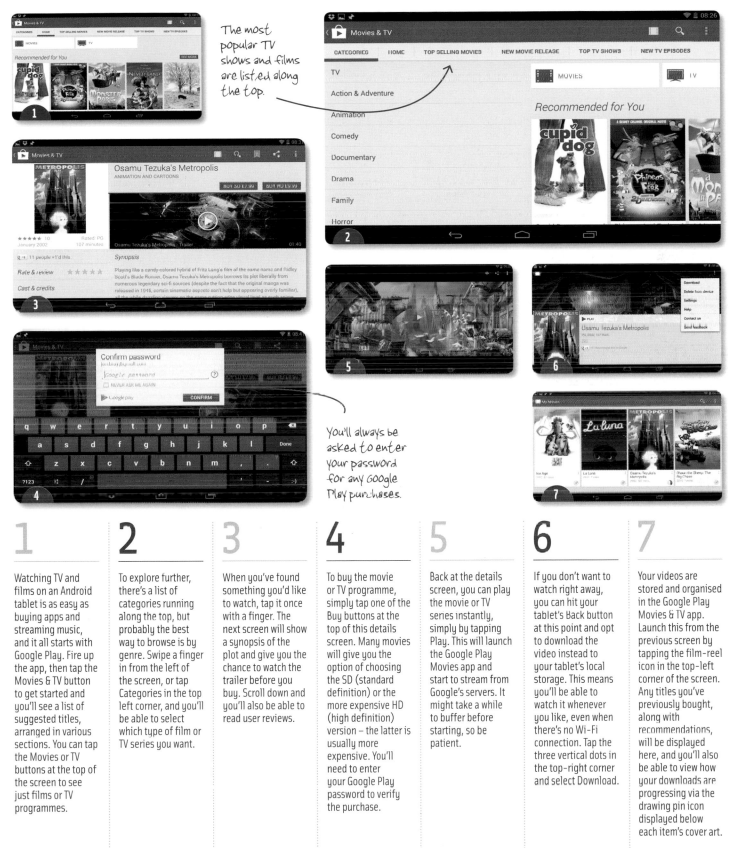

The most popular TV shows and films are listed along the top.

You'll always be asked to enter your password for any Google Play purchases.

1

Watching TV and films on an Android tablet is as easy as buying apps and streaming music, and it all starts with Google Play. Fire up the app, then tap the Movies & TV button to get started and you'll see a list of suggested titles, arranged in various sections. You can tap the Movies or TV buttons at the top of the screen to see just films or TV programmes.

2

To explore further, there's a list of categories running along the top, but probably the best way to browse is by genre. Swipe a finger in from the left of the screen, or tap Categories in the top left corner, and you'll be able to select which type of film or TV series you want.

3

When you've found something you'd like to watch, tap it once with a finger. The next screen will show a synopsis of the plot and give you the chance to watch the trailer before you buy. Scroll down and you'll also be able to read user reviews.

4

To buy the movie or TV programme, simply tap one of the Buy buttons at the top of this details screen. Many movies will give you the option of choosing the SD (standard definition) or the more expensive HD (high definition) version – the latter is usually more expensive. You'll need to enter your Google Play password to verify the purchase.

5

Back at the details screen, you can play the movie or TV series instantly, simply by tapping Play. This will launch the Google Play Movies app and start to stream from Google's servers. It might take a while to buffer before starting, so be patient.

6

If you don't want to watch right away, you can hit your tablet's Back button at this point and opt to download the video instead to your tablet's local storage. This means you'll be able to watch it whenever you like, even when there's no Wi-Fi connection. Tap the three vertical dots in the top-right corner and select Download.

7

Your videos are stored and organised in the Google Play Movies & TV app. Launch this from the previous screen by tapping the film-reel icon in the top-left corner of the screen. Any titles you've previously bought, along with recommendations, will be displayed here, and you'll also be able to view how your downloads are progressing via the drawing pin icon displayed below each item's cover art.

ENJOYING MUSIC
Browsing, playing, buying and streaming. There really is no limit to your Android tablet's tuneful talents, so follow our advice and place it at the centre of your musical world

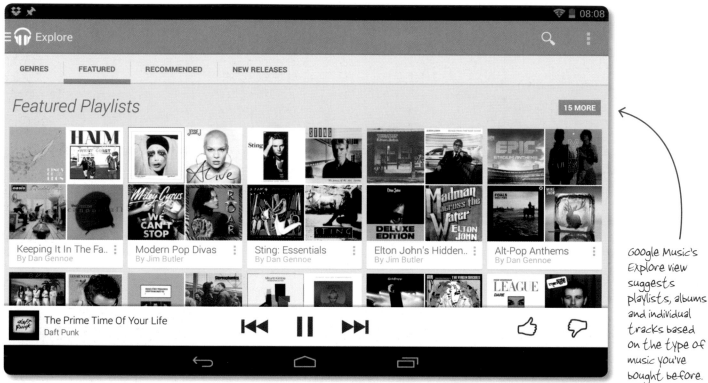

Google Music's Explore view suggests playlists, albums and individual tracks based on the type of music you've bought before.

TIP
The scroll bar on the right-hand side of the screen lets you scroll through your entire music library in one fluid movement.

Android's music facilities are one of its most undersold features. In conjunction with Google Play's music store, you can not only play music on the tablet itself, but also purchase tracks and albums online, stream them from online storage or download them so they can be listened to offline.

The music app itself is a dream to use. It opens up on the Listen Now screen, which shows recently listened to and purchased items, so you don't have to scroll through your whole music library every time you want to listen to something new.

This isn't the only way of viewing tracks, though. A swipe in from the left edge of the screen opens the navigation panel, where the Play Music app's different sections are displayed. To view your entire library by album, artist and

song title, tap the My Library option. There's also a full-blown keyword search tool, and creating playlists is a doddle too.

Once you've set your tracks playing, you can pop off and do something else – browse your email, or read a few pages of your latest Kindle ebook – while the music continues to play in the background. The controls are still close at hand, though: pull the Notifications menu down from the top-left corner of the screen and you'll see a summary box at the top, complete with the album cover, song name and artist, plus skip and pause track controls.

To stretch your tablet's musical legs, you're going to need to add a few more tracks than the small handful of samples provided. You can do this in a number of ways. The

simplest method is to drag and drop folders full of music tracks straight to your tablet's Music folder. Just plug in the tablet and use the file browser on your computer to transfer the tracks you want to listen to (see p16).

PLAY THE MARKET
Another option is to buy and download music straight to the tablet. The easiest to use is Google's own Play Store, with a huge range of albums and music available at very reasonable prices. The walkthrough on the right shows you how to get started.

There are all sorts of apps in the Android Market that let you do even more. You can stream music using subscription services such as Spotify, or listen to tracks from another laptop, PC or Mac over your home network without having to copy them first.

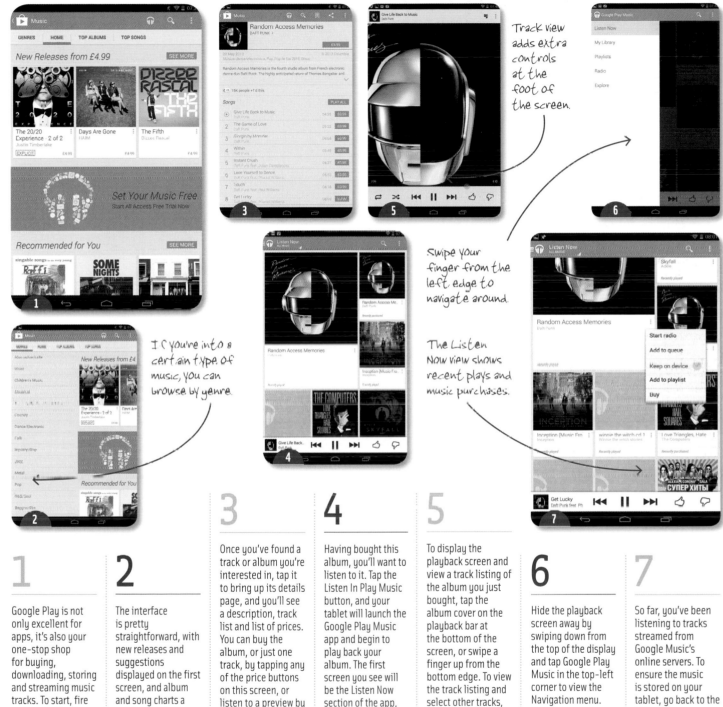

Track view adds extra controls at the foot of the screen.

If you're into a certain type of music, you can browse by genre.

Swipe your finger from the left edge to navigate around.

The Listen Now view shows recent plays and music purchases.

1

Google Play is not only excellent for apps, it's also your one-stop shop for buying, downloading, storing and streaming music tracks. To start, fire up Google Play from the app drawer and tap the Music button at the top of the screen.

2

The interface is pretty straightforward, with new releases and suggestions displayed on the first screen, and album and song charts a quick swipe to the right away. You can also swipe left to browse by genre, or tap the magnifying icon at the top of the screen to search by keyword.

3

Once you've found a track or album you're interested in, tap it to bring up its details page, and you'll see a description, track list and list of prices. You can buy the album, or just one track, by tapping any of the price buttons on this screen, or listen to a preview by tapping the track title.

4

Having bought this album, you'll want to listen to it. Tap the Listen In Play Music button, and your tablet will launch the Google Play Music app and begin to play back your album. The first screen you see will be the Listen Now section of the app, where recent purchases and played-back tracks are displayed at the top, and other music is shown below.

5

To display the playback screen and view a track listing of the album you just bought, tap the album cover on the playback bar at the bottom of the screen, or swipe a finger up from the bottom edge. To view the track listing and select other tracks, tap the musical note icon in the top-right corner.

6

Hide the playback screen away by swiping down from the top of the display and tap Google Play Music in the top-left corner to view the Navigation menu. From here, you can jump quickly between the app's different sections. My Library and Listen Now will be the sections you use the most.

7

So far, you've been listening to tracks streamed from Google Music's online servers. To ensure the music is stored on your tablet, go back to the Listen Now screen, tap the three vertical dots beneath and to the right of the album you want to keep, and select "Keep on device". Now you can listen wherever you want.

READING BOOKS & MAGS *That fantastic tablet screen isn't just for apps and games; it also works brilliantly with the latest books and magazines. Here we show you how to find and subscribe to PC Pro magazine*

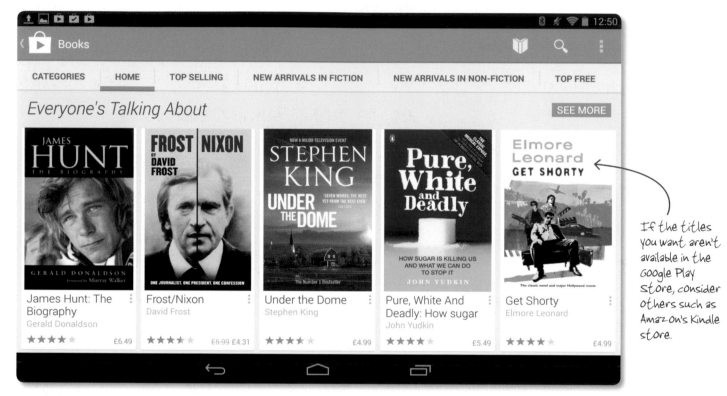

If the titles you want aren't available in the Google Play Store, consider others such as Amazon's Kindle store.

TIP
Make full use of Google's 30-day free trials. If you don't like a magazine, just cancel before you're charged.

From the time of their first arrival, tablets were seen as an exciting possible future for the magazine industry, but few would have predicted they'd also become a popular choice for avid book readers.

The Google Play Store has changed all that for Android tablets. It now has dedicated Books and Magazines sections alongside the usual Apps and Games, and it's a simple process to purchase either a book or a single issue of a magazine, or to subscribe to read a particular publication every time a new issue arrives.

Reading books on a shiny, backlit tablet screen might not have quite the comfort of an E Ink reader like the Kindle, but it has some major advantages. You can zoom in on text and quickly look things up online, and tablets can also display illustrations.

The high-resolution colour screens of today's Android tablets are great for books, and they hold even more potential for magazines. The publishing industry has risen to the challenge with some fantastic tablet-specific designs and interactive features. Magazines on a tablet can have video embedded right on the page next to the text, as well as images you can rotate and zoom. Even if a publisher hasn't made a special tablet version of a magazine, you can usually still buy a standard edition that's made up of digital replicas of every physical page.

Best of all, like all other downloaded content, Google Play keeps all of your purchases in one easily browsed and searched collection, lets you know when new issues are out, and even puts your latest purchases right on your tablet's homescreen for easy access.

TRY BEFORE YOU BUY
You may be wondering how you pay for all this content. It's simple enough with a one-off purchase – you use the same credit card you linked to your Google account to buy apps and games – but what about subscriptions?

Thankfully, it's all very simple to set up a magazine subscription on your Android tablet and, unlike Apple, Google also makes it easy to change your mind.

Subscriptions aren't billed straight away, even though you can download the latest magazine issue immediately upon setting one up. Instead, Google offers a 30-day trial period, during which you're free to browse the magazine and read any or all of its articles. If you later decide to cancel, you can. Otherwise, the first payment will be taken from your account on the date specified when you subscribe.

1

Setting up a magazine subscription is easy in Android. Just go to the Magazines section of the Play Store, either by opening the store and navigation to the section, or by using the Play Magazines shortcut in the app drawer. You'll be greeted by any magazines you own, but for now click Shop.

2

You can browse through the popular and recommended titles, but for this walkthrough we're going to subscribe to *PC Pro* magazine. We tap the search icon and type "pc pro" to bring up our chosen magazine. Tap that to go to the magazine's download page.

3

There will be two buttons at the top of this page. You can buy a single issue for a set price or – assuming the option is offered by your chosen title – you can subscribe. Click the Subscribe button to bring up the options: for *PC Pro*, you can either have the payment taken monthly for each issue or pay for a year up-front.

4

If you don't already have a credit card on your account, you'll need to enter your details here. Pay close attention to the date of your first payment – that's your free 30-day trial window.

Searching for a book or magazine will also bring up results from other sections of Google Play.

5

Once you've completed payment, the Subscribe button on the magazine page will change to a Read button. Tap that to open your new magazine. It will take a short while to download all the high-quality pages, so you might not be able to start reading immediately.

6

And there's your magazine. Depending on your tablet's screen size and resolution, you might have to zoom in and scroll around the page to see everything in detail. When you zoom in on text, tap the View Text button that appears to see a text-only version of the current article.

7

Don't like your magazine choice? As long as you're within your 30-day trial period, you can still back out and it won't cost you a penny. Back on your Magazines library homescreen, tap the settings icon in the top-right corner and choose Manage subscriptions to easily cancel.

You can get plenty of information about a title before you spend any cash.

Once you have your magazine, you can swipe across pages and zoom in to read text more easily.

ESSENTIAL APPS *for entertainment*

Wondering which apps to download next? These will allow you to make the most of your tablet's multimedia capabilities, and should be the first you download

Plex
Price: £3.21

Moving video from your computer onto an Android tablet usually involves converting the file, then copying it into the tablet's video folder. With Plex, you can stream your video files straight from your PC or Mac – just install the accompanying helper application on your computer, point the Plex app at your machine's IP address and it will stream everything from Full HD camcorder clips to recorded TV files, straight to the screen of your tablet. It works remotely, too, if you're prepared to fiddle with your router settings.

Shazam
Price: Free

Never suffer the agony of grasping unsuccessfully for an old song title buried deep in your memory. Shazam is your new pub buddy who knows everything there is to know about music. When you have a track you don't recognise, just fire up Shazam and hold your tablet up to the nearest speaker. The software will analyse the track in real time before sending over the artist and title, a stack load of information and often even a link to buy the song from an online retailer.

SoundCloud
Price: Free

SoundCloud puts a world of audio at your fingertips. Members can record and upload their own music, DJ mixes, sound effects or audio recordings and share them with other users, which also makes it an invaluable resource for collaborating with fellow music-makers around the world. SoundCloud is also popular with professional musicians, artists, record labels and DJs, who regularly share exclusive tracks, upload DJ mixes or demo their latest releases.

Spotify
Price: Free

Why buy your music when you can just pay a monthly fee to access more than you could ever listen to in a lifetime? Okay, you don't really own any of it, but even the free version of Spotify can keep you entertained for a long time, and not just on your tablet, as you can use Spotify on near enough any PC, Mac or portable device out there. Stick to the latest charts, browse the recommendations or try out playlists created by other users. It's the more social way to expand your musical horizons.

Xbox SmartGlass
Price: Free

You'll see various devices and services that turn a tablet into a remote control throughout this book, and there's even an official app from Microsoft that lets you control your Xbox. Along with simple dashboard navigation, you can use your tablet's keyboard to search and enter passwords, pause and rewind videos, track your Achievements when you're not at your Xbox and even – with supported games – use your tablet as a second screen to add more to the experience.

Netflix
Price: Free

Unless you've been living under a rock for the past year or two, you'll be aware of Netflix, the video-on-demand service that's taking the TV world by storm. As well as some of the most popular shows available, it has exclusives such as *Breaking Bad* and even its own original productions with some big names involved. Watch *House of Cards* if you don't believe us. The app is free, but it will cost you a monthly fee of £5.99 to access unlimited TV shows and movies, in HD if your screen and internet connection can handle it.

Steam
Price: Free

Don't get your hopes up: the official Steam app for Android won't let you play your PC games on your tablet – at least not just yet. What it will do is give you full access to your profile and friends, so you can browse the community, chat about the latest games, catch up on news and – let's be honest, this is what you're really after – splash your cash in the regular massive Steam sales without having to fire up your PC. Just pick up a game on your tablet on the way home.

FL Studio Mobile
Price: £12.95

The iPad might seem to have the monopoly on music production apps, but FL Studio Mobile tips the balance back in Android's favour. It isn't cheap, but provides an incredibly in-depth audio mixing experience, allowing you to effortlessly create tracks using a stunning range of more than 130 instruments. It can also connect with the desktop version of FL Studio, which is one of the most popular PC music creation tools around.

OnLive
Price: Free

OnLive allows you to play cutting-edge games on your tablet without having to shell out for an expensive console or PC. It's a cloud-based system that streams the game to your device from OnLive's remote servers, and amazingly there's little to no slowdown or latency. You can even use Bluetooth controllers for the authentic experience. Many free demos are available, but games can also be purchased outright or you can subscribe for unlimited access to selected titles.

IMDb
Price: Free

This is the perfect app for armchair movie enthusiasts and those who get embroiled in pub arguments about which actor starred in which film. IMDb has photos, trailers, user reviews and a seemingly limitless mountain of data about almost every film ever made. You can browse new releases, consult the career of your favourite Hollywood star or place your personal vote for the best cinematic experience of all time. Sadly, popcorn isn't included.

GAMING FOR TABLETS
You'll be amazed at how much fun you can have with an Android tablet. With console-quality games and hundreds of free time wasters, you'll never be bored again

There's no longer any need to buy a dedicated gaming device. Your tablet will do everything a Nintendo 3DS or Sony PlayStation Vita can, but on a larger, higher-quality screen. The advanced hardware packed into today's Android 4 tablets means effects and 3D graphics look incredible. Nor is that the only advantage of owning a power-packed Android tablet.

As with standard apps, games are much cheaper than they are on a games console, portable or not, with prices starting low and rarely topping around £5. Many great titles are available completely free. Google curates the best and most popular in the Games section of the Play Store.

What can you expect from the latest tablet titles? A lot. As well as great graphics, the best games use the touchscreen to more naturally control the play, while some rely on the accelerometer in your tablet for motion controls, although this kind of play can be very hit and miss.

If you already own an Android smartphone, you may find some of the games you've bought also run on tablets, in which case they'll often be waiting for download in the Google Play Store. And there are thousands more great games just waiting to be discovered and downloaded to your homescreen, just as we described back in Chapter 1.

GRAPHICAL POWER
The age and price of your tablet will go a long way towards determining the kind of games you can play. If you buy a brand-new tablet like the Google Nexus 7, you can pretty much take your pick of any demanding 3D game in the store. But if you're trundling along on an older device, or opt to save money with a budget tablet, you may find its graphics chip is too weak to handle the latest games smoothly. They may still run, but in scenes with a lot of action you may see the gameplay slow down to sometimes unplayable levels. There's not a lot you can do about this, as the core specifications of a tablet aren't upgradeable.

The one thing you can do to avoid it happening at all is to choose the right tablet. Be sure to read all of our reviews in Chapter 5, where we talk about each tablet's performance, particularly in the latest games. If we mention 3D gaming issues and gaming is a priority for you, it's best to look elsewhere.

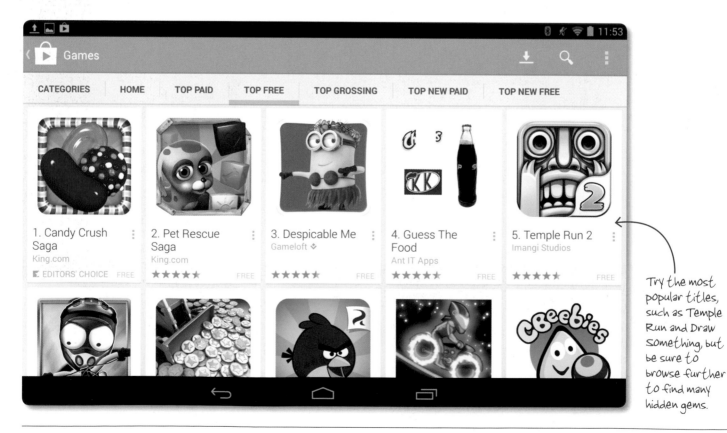

Try the most popular titles, such as Temple Run and Draw Something, but be sure to browse further to find many hidden gems.

Everything you'll ever need to know about **Windows 8**

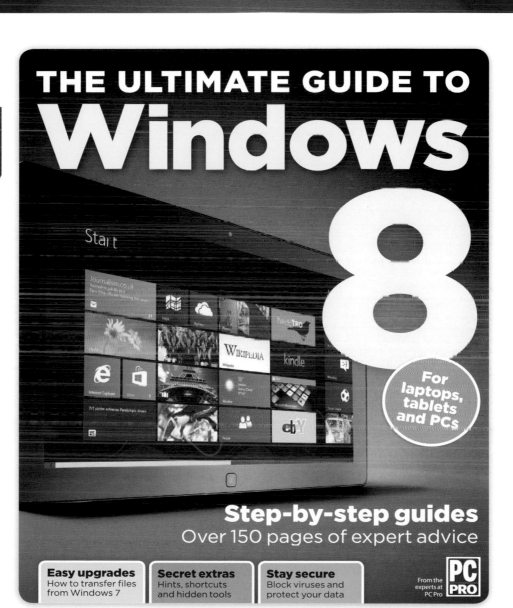

GAME REVIEWS *Our pick of the top titles*

There are so many games and, with new ones being released every day, it can be difficult to know where to start. Here's a selection of our favourites

The Room
Price: 69p

If you haven't been in The Room yet, you're in for a treat. Few puzzle games can match its glorious sense of mystery, as you explore a box on a table – it's much more interesting than it sounds – looking for clues as to how to get inside. Each solved puzzle triggers another, until before long this simple box has become an elaborate layered maze of drawers, hidden compartments and strange symbols. As you get deeper into the puzzle, the tools and tricks get more complex, and if you turn off the hints you'll be punching the air as you solve the last few puzzles. An absolute triumph.

Candy Crush Saga
Price: Free

In the ridiculously addictive Candy Crush, your job is to destroy a grid of sweets by matching up their colours. It sounds like pretty straightforward puzzle-gaming stuff, but there are over 400 levels to get through, with a wide array of power-ups that keep the game feeling fresh as you get further and further along. It's a free game but, as is becoming more and more common, it starts putting stupidly hard levels in the way later on, which, of course, you can pay to make easier.

Plague Inc
Price: Free

At first glance, Plague Inc looks complicated, and in some ways it is, but don't let that put you off. This marvellous game is about disease; and not curing it, but spreading it. You choose a virus and a starting country, then set about evolving your symptoms and transmission methods to try and spread to nearby countries, then develop resistances to counter the cure research that soon starts as you begin to wipe out the human race. That's your overall goal; achieving it isn't easy.

Asphalt 8
Price: 69p

Where Real Racing 3 goes for realism, Asphalt has always been about pure, over-the-top arcade fun. Perform dramatic aerial stunts off ramps as you tear around a variety of inventive tracks in real-life high-performance cars, such as the Bugatti Veyron and Pagani Zonda R. A career mode and the ability to race against the ghosts of your previous best laps will keep you coming back for more, and the team keep adding new game modes to keep things interesting.

Plants vs Zombies
Price: 69p

It really shouldn't work, but somehow it does. This tower defence game sees a steady flow of zombies entering your garden, and you have to stop them with... plants, obviously. Different plants have different attacks and effects, and the key is to line them up cleverly so range-attack plants sit behind more melee-style plants. With a lovely variety to the zombie hordes, and a cartoonish style that masks the deceptively demanding gameplay, it's a must-have.

Temple Run 2
Price: Free

The endless runner genre is now hugely popular, but Temple Run really started the craze. It's a very simple game: your character runs forward automatically at all times, and you have to tilt your device to shift him left and right on his narrow runway to avoid obstacles and collect gems, and swipe left and right on the screen to turn corners as they arrive. The goal is just to keep running for as long as possible, which gets extremely challenging after a few minutes. Upgrades between runs help.

Real Racing 3
Price: Free

Those who think of Android tablets as mainly for light puzzle games will surely be astonished by the console-quality graphics in this action-packed racing game from EA. Drive some of your favourite real-life cars on immaculately recreated tracks, and jostle with rivals to pick up victories that let you improve your car before the next race. It's exciting stuff, but be warned: it takes up over a gigabyte of your storage, so might be best avoided on some tablets.

Fruit Ninja
Price: Free

One of those games that, like Angry Birds and Temple Run, seems to be a default choice on every tablet, Fruit Ninja is nevertheless a great way to while away a short tube journey. It's not exactly complicated: fruit flies up in the air, and you have to slice it in half with your sword. As you progress, the basic gameplay is complicated by bombs and other best-avoided items that mingle with the fruit to confuse and confound you. There's a fun two-player mode, too.

N.O.V.A. 3
Price: £4.99

If you want to go down the big blockbuster shooter route, they don't come much louder than N.O.V.A. 3, which stands for Near Orbit Vanguard Alliance. It takes up a huge 2GB of your tablet's storage, but for that you get console-quality graphics, an epic single-player story and a full 12-player multiplayer mode. Controlling first-person shooters on a tablet has never been ideal, but if you can get your thumbs around it you'll have a lot of fun with N.O.V.A. 3.

Terraria
Price: Free

Exploration is key in Terraria, a retro platform game that sucks you in as you delve deeper and deeper into its amazing world. Your little avatar must dig for materials to craft increasingly complex items, which help him progress further and further from his starting point in the forest. Yes, it has an element of Minecraft about it, but it's delightfully put together, and it's a game that really rewards the patient gamer. Be warned: it's not the easiest game to get into.

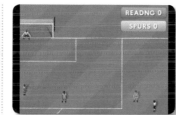

New Star Soccer
Price: £1.99

While lots of the big developers focus on bombastic blockbusters with lifelike graphics, a huge number of people ignore them to play this Sensible Soccer-esque football sim. Work your way up the ranks from non-league to the Champions League by managing your fitness and spending your money wisely, and most of all by taking to the pitch and scoring spectacular goals. The simple graphics and basic swipe-to-shoot mechanics make it easy to pick up and play, and become addicted.

Super Hexagon
Price: £1.99

And now for something completely different. Super Hexagon is about as simple as a game can be to look at, and each game lasts barely a few seconds unless you're really good at it, but it's that quick-play design that makes it so incredibly compelling. You're a tiny triangle and, as the hypnotic shapes close in, to a pulsating electronic soundtrack, you simply slide left and right to manoeuvre through the gaps. It sounds simple; it's practically impossible, even on easy mode.

Angry Birds
Price: Free

No gaming guide would be complete without Angry Birds and its many spin-offs. The goal is simple: using a catapult, launch your birds across the screen to kill the pigs. You enemies lurk behind walls of wood, ice and stone, and it requires birds of different abilities to crack their resolve: from ice-breaking cluster birds, to boomerang birds that can spin around corners. Fiendishly addictive, and with regular, new updates to keep you well and truly hooked.

In this chapter

ANDROID FOR TABLETS
STAYING CONNECTED

Email, instant messaging, social networking, internet telephony, browsing the web – you name it, you can do it on a tablet. In this chapter, we reveal just how powerful a communications tool an Android tablet can be, how it can help bring you, your friends and family closer together, and how it might just revolutionise the way you use the internet.

BROWSING THE WEB
Android's integrated web browser is powerful and easy to use, but you'll need to learn a few tricks to make the most of it. Here we reveal some of the features that will help you master the internet

Android 4 comes with the Chrome browser, so many desktop users will be right at home.

TIP

If a site opens in mobile phone view, it's easy to change. Tick the box for "Request desktop site" in the browser settings.

The internet is now so central to our lives that we often take the software we use to access it for granted. That's as it should be, and Android 4's built-in web browser makes the task more of a pleasure than most.

That's because it's Google Chrome, the same browser many of us use on our PCs and laptops on a daily basis, which makes it very simple to get going. It's all based around tabs, which allow you to have several web pages open at once, which is handy for keeping on top of the football results while putting together the weekly shop! A single tap is all that's required to add a new one, and flicking between them is just as simple.

Android's multitouch gestures mean you can scroll up and down web pages with an effortless flick of the finger. You can pinch two fingers together to zoom out for an overview, and pinch them

together again to zoom in. You can also drag pages about as if you were shuffling paper around on your desk.

ADDRESS CODE
The browser's address bar is where all the work gets done. As well as using it to enter addresses in the normal way, you can also type search terms directly into the same box. Once you get used to this approach, it becomes the natural way to search Google.

And if you really hate typing, there's an option to search by speaking into your tablet's microphone; look for the microphone icon and tap it when it appears. You can add bookmarks for your favourite pages with a tap of the finger, and browse through the pages you've visited recently. If you want to browse without leaving tracks, just open a new incognito tab.

If a site has a mobile version that will be loaded automatically, but if you prefer the layout of the desktop site, just tap the settings icon in the top-right corner and make sure "Request desktop site" is checked.

NO FLASH
You may be disappointed to discover that Google has dropped support for Adobe's Flash technology. Flash is the standard that allows websites to play video content directly from the web page, and many advanced websites also rely on it to power graphics-heavy interactive elements. You'll need to use apps to watch video from the BBC, for example, as the browser will give you an error message. There are third-party browsers in the Play Store that will bring back that Flash support, but expect to pay for them.

WALKTHROUGH *Tapping the web browser's hidden powers*

1
Android 4's Chrome browser is very much like its desktop counterpart, and there's no better example than its use of tabs. These allow you to have more than one web page open at a time. Simply tap a tab to switch to that web page, or press the plus icon on the right to add a new one.

2
The Quick Settings menu in the Chrome browser has some useful options. Some sites may open in a cutdown mobile mode as they've detected your tablet browser. If you prefer the full desktop website, tick Request desktop site and refresh the page.

3
Tapping small links on a touchscreen can be tricky, particularly if you have chubby fingers. Thankfully, a tap will often bring up a zoomed area so you can choose the link you want more precisely.

4
Accessed from within the Quick Settings pull-down menu, the full Settings menu lets you change advanced features such as whether cookies are collected or plugins enabled, or whether Google will translate pages.

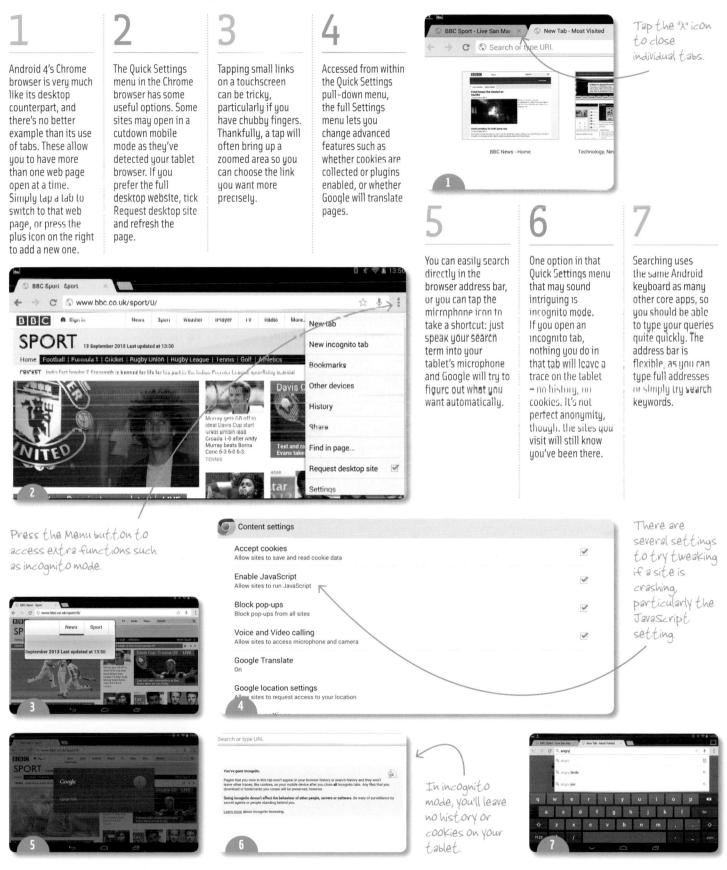

Tap the "x" icon to close individual tabs.

5
You can easily search directly in the browser address bar, or you can tap the microphone icon to take a shortcut: just speak your search term into your tablet's microphone and Google will try to figure out what you want automatically.

6
One option in that Quick Settings menu that may sound intriguing is incognito mode. If you open an incognito tab, nothing you do in that tab will leave a trace on the tablet – no history, no cookies. It's not perfect anonymity, though: the sites you visit will still know you've been there.

7
Searching uses the same Android keyboard as many other core apps, so you should be able to type your queries quite quickly. The address bar is flexible, as you can type full addresses or simply try search keywords.

Press the Menu button to access extra functions such as incognito mode.

There are several settings to try tweaking if a site is crashing, particularly the JavaScript setting.

In incognito mode, you'll leave no history or cookies on your tablet.

MASTERING EMAIL

Android 4's excellent apps make it so easy to keep on top of your mail that you may find you never go back to using your laptop again. We explain how to take full advantage using Gmail

TIP

Can't find an email? The Gmail app searches messages on Google's servers, as well as your locally stored email.

Social-networking services such as Facebook and Twitter may be dominating much of our time as well as our social lives, but you're still likely to spend more time typing emails than almost anything else. Fortunately, the ability to do this effortlessly lies at the core of Android 4.

In Chapter 1, we discovered that in order to unlock the full potential of your Android tablet you need a Google account. That's taken care of during the setup process (see p15), and when you fire up your tablet's Gmail app for the very first time you'll find it already populated with all your messages.

You'll also find that Android's core email application – which is in the app drawer under the Gmail icon – makes reading and responding to your emails an absolute pleasure.

It makes use of Google's revamped approach to the inbox. Emails are automatically filtered into one of five categories, so you'll no longer have to sift through promotions and spam to get to your important mails. If you find something has been incorrectly assigned, just tap Move To and choose the correct category.

GETTING AROUND

Tap the Gmail icon in the top-left to bring up the Inbox menu on the left side, and your chosen folder will appear on the right. Tap on the message subject and the body of your email will appear, sweeping in from the right. An index of your email remains in a pane on the left, so you can quickly browse your messages with a tap of your finger. To return to the main overview, you tap

the Gmail icon at the top of the screen.

Just as with your web-based Gmail account, emails are displayed by default in "conversation" view, grouping all messages with the same subject line together, helping you to keep track of lengthy email exchanges.

If you've bought the tablet for the whole household, you can add multiple Gmail accounts for each member of the family if you like. Switching between them is simple: tap the email address in the top right-hand corner of the screen and a menu will appear listing all your Gmail accounts. You then choose which account you want to access.

It's not just Gmail that's made simple. Android Email app, which is effectively the same thing as Gmail, lets you add anything from your Outlook work email to your Yahoo or Hotmail accounts.

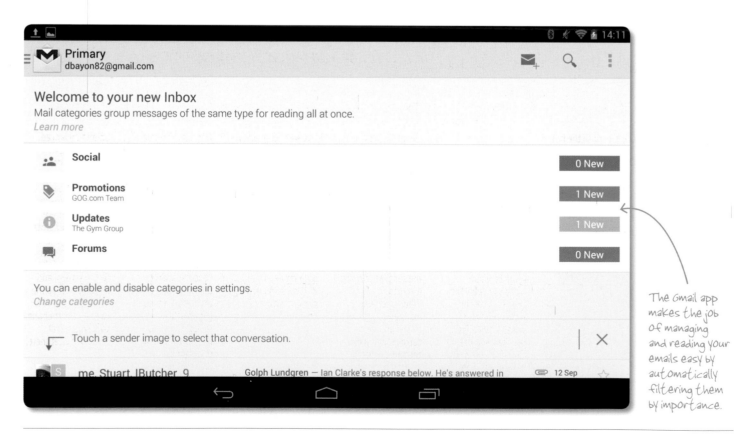

The Gmail app makes the job of managing and reading your emails easy by automatically filtering them by importance.

Switching between multiple Gmail accounts is simple: just tap the address in the top left corner.

Gmail uses the standard Android keyboard, so you can dictate messages if you want to.

If you want Gmail to double-check when you delete an email, the option can be turned on in General Settings.

1

Gmail's new inbox is a great improvement to how messages are filed. When messages arrive, they're automatically put into one of five containers, with only Primary messages deemed important enough by default to trigger an alert. If a message arrives and goes into the wrong pot, just drag it into the correct one and Gmail will learn over time how you like things done.

2

Open one of the five containers and you'll see your mail in a neat list, with different senders assigned different colours and icons. Tap any message to open the mail in the full window.

3

Opening a mail changes the view. The list of mails in your inbox shrinks to a column down the left, while the content of the mail opens in a large window to the right. Once you've read it, tap the Reply, Reply All or Forward buttons to deal with your mail without leaving the reading pane. Alternatively, tap the favourite icon so you can easily find it later.

4

The mails in your inbox remain in view down the left column, and Gmail does something clever with them. You'll only see one mail from each person; that's because conversations with the same sender are grouped together. When you open that mail, you'll also see all the previous correspondence in the same place.

5

Composing an email is simple, as Gmail uses exactly the same Android keyboard as most of the other core apps. All the same features apply: tap the microphone button to dictate a message, or swipe through your letter to build words without having to type individual keys.

6

This being Google, the search bar is, of course, a very powerful tool. Searching for a keyword will bring up results from your inbox, sent items and any other folder you've created. It can search in headers, addresses and even within the body of an email, so you should be able to find anything as long as it's still in your inbox.

7

Gmail's advanced settings let you tweak all sorts of useful bits and pieces. You can choose whether a swipe will delete messages, whether sender image is enabled, whether messages shrink to fit the screen, and much more. Tap the settings icon in the top-right corner and choose General Settings to get there.

Yahoo! Mobile > Yahoo! Mobile > Communications > Yahoo! Mail

Setting up IMAP on your mobile device

Last Updated: September 30, 2010

Text Size: A A **A**

To set up IMAP on your mobile device please use these settings

- Incoming Server - imap.mail.yahoo.com
- Outgoing Server - smtp.mail.yahoo.com
- Incoming Port - 993 (requires SSL)
- Outgoing Port - 465 (requires SSL/TLS)
- Username: full email address (for example, bill@yahoo.com or bill@rocketmail.com)
- Password: the password you login to Yahoo! with.

If you are having trouble setting up IMAP on your mobile device we recommend reviewing your phones instruction manual or contacting your mobile provider for support.

Make sure you write down all the details in this step; if you miss anything out, the process will probably fail.

Add an account
Corporate
Email
Google

Account setup
Email account
You can set up email for most accounts in just a few steps.
Email address

Account setup
Account type
What type of account is this?
POP3
IMAP
Exchange
Previous

You can also use your tablet to receive outlook-based work email. Tap the Exchange button to set it up; you may need the details from your IT department.

1

You don't need to stick with Gmail, as your Android tablet can handle accounts from many different types of email provider. First, you'll need to gather all your account details together: your username, password and the details of your service provider's email servers. Here we're going to be adding a Yahoo mail account: you'll find these details by logging in and searching the help section for "setting up IMAP".

2

To add a new email account, launch the Android 4 Settings menu: on the desktop, drag down from the top-right edge of the screen and choose Settings. Scroll down to the Accounts section and select the Add account, then choose Email from the following box.

3

On the next screen, you'll be asked for your username and password. Enter those details, hit Next, and the tablet will attempt to look up the correct settings and set up the email account automatically. If you're lucky, this will work first time and you can skip straight to Step 7. If not, press "Manual setup".

Account setup
Server settings
Domain\Username   \test
Password   •••••••••
Previous

Account settings
Account options
Inbox checking frequency   Every 15 minutes
Send email from this account by default.
Notify me when email arrives.
Sync email from this account.
Automatically download attachments when connected to Wi-Fi

Non-Gmail mail arrives in a separate Email app, although it has similar features to the main Gmail app.

4

This is where you choose the account type. The options are quite cryptic, but most third-party email providers will offer both POP3 and IMAP email connections. It's best to go with IMAP if you have a choice, as this supports more advanced options such as folders. Choose your option to progress to the next stage.

5

On the "Incoming server settings" page, check the details against those you wrote down in Step 1. In this case, the details are wrong: we're going to change the IMAP server address to the correct one by adding ".mail" between "imap" and ".yahoo", and we're going to change the security type to SSL. Hit Next, check the SMTP server details are correct, change the security settings to SSL, and tap Next once again.

6

The last step is to set your account options. This isn't a very important email address, so we're going to tell the tablet to check for new email only once every 15 minutes. You can set this interval to a longer or shorter period by pressing the small downwards arrow. Tap Next to finish.

7

You're all done now. Confusingly, however, you won't find your newly set up email account in the default Gmail application. You'll need to launch the app drawer (on the desktop, tap the circle with the dots inside) and look for the email icon. Mail from your newly added account will arrive here.

Calculator Calendar Camera Chrome Clock
Drive Earth Email Gallery Gmail
Google+ Hangouts Keep Maps Messenger

USING GOOGLE+

Google+ isn't just another social network. In addition to posting messages, you can use it as a store for your photographs and videos, and it can even be used to keep in touch in real-time

F acebook and Twitter are impossible to ignore in the modern world, but you may not be quite so familiar with Google's own social network: Google+.

On the surface, it's just another social network to communicate with friends and family. You can post messages, just as you can with Facebook and Twitter, although they're not limited in length. You can upload photos, videos and links. And your Google+ contacts can comment on or +1 (the Google+ equivalent of a Facebook Like) whatever you post.

CIRCLES OF CONTROL

Unlike other social networks, however, Google+ gives you complete control over who your posts go to in the first place – a concept known as Circles.

Circles give you a way of organising your contacts, so when you start with Google+ you have a Circle for Friends, for Family, for Acquaintances, and one for people you simply want to Follow.

It's also possible to set up your own, custom Circles, so you could have a Circle for work colleagues, for example. Whenever you post to Google+, you then have the choice of whether to make it Public – like you do when you post on Twitter – to share it with only people in your Circles, or restrict it even further by sharing it only with one of your Circles. With Google+, you can also post to individual contacts, or a combination of circles and contacts.

Google+ gives you more control than any other social network, and the Google+ app on your Android tablet makes it child's play to set up and use.

THE GOOGLE+ X FACTOR

There's much more to Google+ than just posting and commenting, though. You can use it to automatically back up every photo and video on your tablet, and then access them on your laptop and smartphone, and share them wherever you want.

It's a good Skype alternative, too, to make video calls. And with Google+'s Hangouts, you're not restricted to calls between only two people; you can set up free video conference calls with three, four or even more people.

Google+ offers the richest set of social networking features on your tablet, but you can use Facebook and Twitter, too. Turn the page for a walkthrough on how to set up your accounts and make the best use of what your Android tablet has to offer.

TIP

Made a typo? There's no need to worry, since you can edit Google+ posts after they've been posted.

Google+ is your tablet's built-in social networking tool and boasts some powerful features

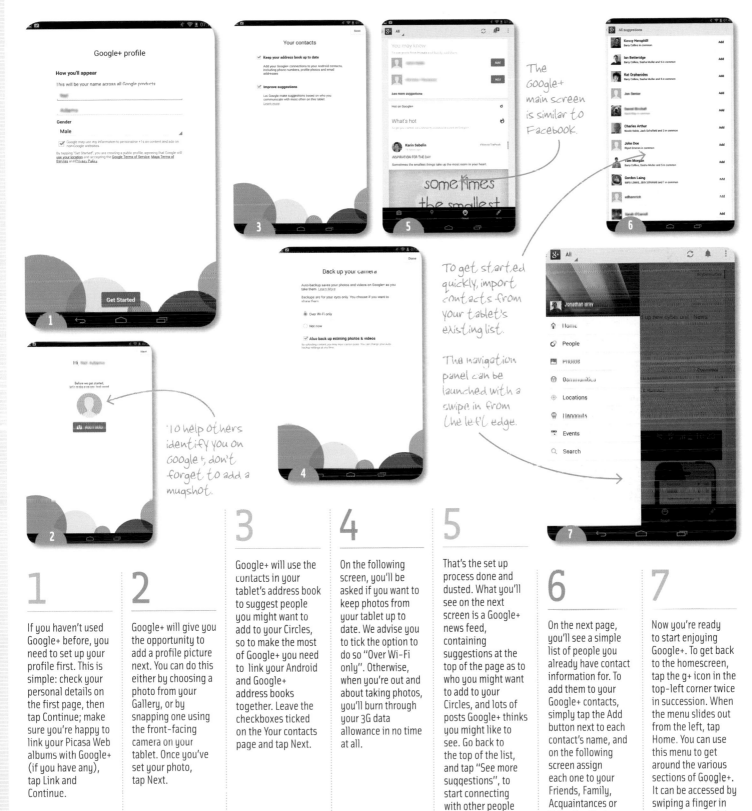

The Google+ main screen is similar to Facebook.

To get started quickly, import contacts from your tablet's existing list.

The navigation panel can be launched with a swipe in from the left edge.

To help others identify you on Google+, don't forget to add a mugshot.

1

If you haven't used Google+ before, you need to set up your profile first. This is simple: check your personal details on the first page, then tap Continue; make sure you're happy to link your Picasa Web albums with Google+ (if you have any), tap Link and Continue.

2

Google+ will give you the opportunity to add a profile picture next. You can do this either by choosing a photo from your Gallery, or by snapping one using the front-facing camera on your tablet. Once you've set your photo, tap Next.

3

Google+ will use the contacts in your tablet's address book to suggest people you might want to add to your Circles, so to make the most of Google+ you need to link your Android and Google+ address books together. Leave the checkboxes ticked on the Your contacts page and tap Next.

4

On the following screen, you'll be asked if you want to keep photos from your tablet up to date. We advise you to tick the option to do so "Over Wi-Fi only". Otherwise, when you're out and about taking photos, you'll burn through your 3G data allowance in no time at all.

5

That's the set up process done and dusted. What you'll see on the next screen is a Google+ news feed, containing suggestions at the top of the page as to who you might want to add to your Circles, and lots of posts Google+ thinks you might like to see. Go back to the top of the list, and tap "See more suggestions", to start connecting with other people on Google+.

6

On the next page, you'll see a simple list of people you already have contact information for. To add them to your Google+ contacts, simply tap the Add button next to each contact's name, and on the following screen assign each one to your Friends, Family, Acquaintances or Following Circles.

7

Now you're ready to start enjoying Google+. To get back to the homescreen, tap the g+ icon in the top-left corner twice in succession. When the menu slides out from the left, tap Home. You can use this menu to get around the various sections of Google+. It can be accessed by swiping a finger in from the edge of the screen, too.

You can add your current location to any tweet.

If you already have a Twitter account, sign into your account using the button on the right.

Your profile lists recent tweets, photos and who's following you.

1

To start using Twitter on your Android tablet, you're going to first have to install the official Twitter app via Google Play. Fire up Google Play, tap the magnifying glass icon at the top of the screen and type Twitter when the keyboard pops up. Select the Twitter app and tap the green Install button.

2

Once Twitter has finished installing, tap Open. Then, on the Twitter welcome screen, tap the Sign In button in the bottom-right corner (if you don't already have an account, you can sign up for one by tapping the Sign Up button in the bottom-left corner). Enter your Twitter username/email and password on the following screen and tap Sign In.

3

If you'd like to let Twitter use your location to geotag your posts, tap OK (you don't have to if you don't want to), and you'll eventually see a list of tweets arranged in front of you. You can scroll up and down the list to read more and tap individual tweets to see details, such as attached photos, plus who's replied to and retweeted it.

4

At this point, Twitter may ask you if you want to import your contacts from your Android tablet. If this is the first time you've used Twitter, it's a good idea to do this, as it will help you find friends. If you're feeling brave, tap Follow all; however, it's probably sensible to scroll down the list, adding only those people you might be interested in seeing updates from.

5

Posting your first tweet couldn't be simpler. Tap the icon in the top-right corner that looks like a box with a quill pen in it and write your post into the box that comes up next. In the top-right corner, is a character count, which shows you how many characters you have left in your tweet. Remember, each tweet can only be a maximum of 140 characters long.

6

To add a photo to your tweet, you can either tap the camera icon at the bottom to share a snap directly using the camera app, or choose a photo from your Gallery with the photo icon. If you want to add your current location to the tweet, you can do that by tapping the arrow icon. Tap the Tweet button in the top-right to finish.

7

The Twitter homescreen is simple to navigate, with four big icons running along the top displaying different views. The @ option shows tweets where you've been mentioned, the # button shows recent activity and trends, and the head icon displays a personal summary: your profile, Twitter stats, recent tweets and recent photos.

WALKTHROUGH *Using Facebook*

You can sign up for a new Facebook account, or use an existing one.

You can update your status as easily as on the Facebook website.

Facebook has hidden depths revealed with a swipe in from the left.

1
To start using Facebook on your Android tablet, you're going to first have to install the official Facebook app via Google Play. Fire up Google Play, tap the magnifying glass icon at the top of the screen and type Facebook when the keyboard pops up. Select Facebook and tap the green Install button.

2
Once Facebook has finished installing, tap Open, then enter your Facebook email and password on the following screen and tap Log In. These are the credentials you usually use to log into the Facebook website. If you don't already have an account, tap the "Sign up for Facebook" link at the very bottom of the screen.

3
The Facebook app will now launch and you'll be able to use it, much as you can the website. To fully integrate Facebook with your tablet, however, you're now going to need to go to the Settings menu and change a few small details.

4
Drag a finger down from the top-right corner of the screen (or, on older tablets, tap in the bottom-right corner), then select Settings. On the next screen, scroll down to the Accounts section – about halfway down – and select Facebook.

5
On the following screen, tap the checkbox to the right of the Contacts option, and your Facebook contacts, along with all their details, will now be stored on your tablet alongside your Gmail contacts in the People app.

6
You can now start using Facebook in earnest. Launch the app (it should log in automatically), and you'll see that the most important controls are at the top of the screen. Tap Status to launch the Write Post screen, type your thoughts into the box, add a photo, video or location using the buttons at the bottom, and hit Post.

7
In the top left-hand corner of the main Facebook screen, you'll see an icon in the shape of three horizontal lines. Tap this to access the navigation window, which will slide in from the left-hand side (swiping in a finger from the left edge of the screen works, too). Use this menu to see all of Facebook's various sections.

SECURE YOUR ANDROID TABLET

There will be a lot of sensitive, personal information stored on your Android tablet. Here's how to keep it from prying eyes

05:51

WED, SEPTEMBER 25

New user

To prevent just anyone accessing your tablet, you need to set up security, and Android offers a number of ways you can do this.

TIP
Keep the tablet screen clean. Swiping in the same pattern to unlock it leaves grease, which can be seen under the right light.

Once you've bought and familiarised yourself with your Android tablet, chances are you won't want anyone else getting their hands on it. With email, Twitter, Facebook accounts set up, it's likely to be filled to the brim with personal information that you won't want anybody else rooting around in.

The good news is that there are plenty of ways to protect data on an Android tablet, with the first step being to put a lock on the front door. The simplest way to achieve this is to set up a PIN code: once you've done this, every time you turn on the tablet you'll be required to enter a four-digit number.

You'll find all the settings you need in the main Settings menu in the app drawer, under the Security entry. You'll see plenty more settings to fiddle with

on the following screen, but the one you want is the "Screen lock" entry, which sits at the very top. One selected, you'll find the PIN setup option on the next screen. Setting up a PIN from here is pretty straightforward.

If remembering numbers isn't a strong point, there are other options available. You can use a password to keep your tablet secure. You can use a pattern to unlock your tablet, where you draw a shape on a grid of nine dots to gain access. This can be quicker and easier to enter and is no less secure than a PIN or password. And, if you're really lazy, you can unlock the tablet using facial recognition. However, bear in mind that in darkened environments this system won't work particularly well.

A PIN, password or pattern can prevent the casual thief or opportunist from accessing your data, but if you

want to be sure they won't be able to extract your emails, passwords and other sensitive information if your tablet is lost or stolen, you'll need to use your Android tablet's encryption option.

Encryption works by scrambling all the data stored on the tablet, so it's accessible only from the tablet and by the person (for example, you) who knows the unlock key – be that your PIN or password. Without encryption, any information extracted from the tablet without unlocking it first would be unreadable.

Fortunately, you don't need to be a security expert to set up encryption. Simply tap the "Encrypt tablet" option in the Security menu, then follow the instructions. You'll need the tablet to be fully charged, however, and plugged into the mains, since the encryption process can take some time.

Tracing a pattern to unlock your tablet is easy.

You can switch security methods with a single tap.

Full encryption helps you keep your personal information private.

Using your face to unlock your tablet is surprisingly reliable.

1

The first step in securing your tablet is to go to your tablet's Settings menu, which you'll find in the app drawer. Scroll down until you find the Security option – it's about halfway down the page in the Personal subsection.

2

On the next screen, you'll see a wide variety of different settings, most of which you don't need to worry about. The setting you want is the "Screen lock" entry at the very top of the page, beneath the heading Screen security, with the current setting summarised beneath it. Tap the menu item and move onto the next step.

3

You'll see that the screen lock is set to Slide by default, which isn't secure at all. To enable pattern unlocking – the most convenient and quick method – tap that option in the list.

4

On the next screen, you'll be asked to trace out a pattern with your finger over a grid of nine dots. You can use some or all the dots, trace out as simple or complex a pattern as you like. Tap Continue, trace out the same pattern once again on the following screen and hit Confirm to finish.

5

The next time you switch your tablet off, you'll be presented with a nine-dot grid on the lockscreen. All you need to do to unlock the tablet is to quickly draw the pattern you drew in step 4.

6

Another quick and easy way to lock and unlock your tablet is to use facial recognition. This uses the front-facing camera to take a picture of your face, which is then used to unlock the tablet. To set this up, go back to step 3 and choose "Face unlock".

7

Follow the instructions on the next couple of screens, then hold your tablet at eye level, and line your face up with the guidelines on screen while the front-facing camera takes a snap. Finally, you'll be asked to set up a backup security method in case the facial recognition doesn't work because of poor light, for instance.

ESSENTIAL APPS *for comms and the web*

The default Android apps for email and the web are good, but you can add further
features thanks to a wealth of third-party apps. Here are ten of the best

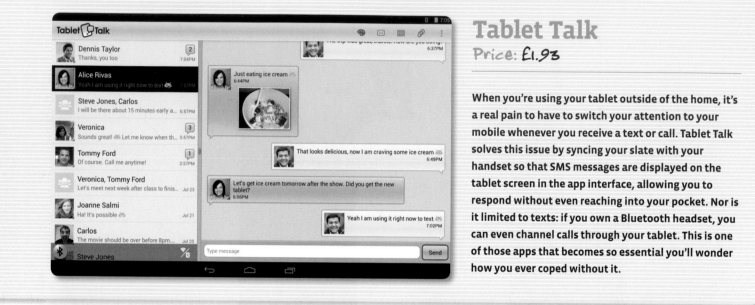

Tablet Talk
Price: £1.93

When you're using your tablet outside of the home, it's
a real pain to have to switch your attention to your
mobile whenever you receive a text or call. Tablet Talk
solves this issue by syncing your slate with your
handset so that SMS messages are displayed on the
tablet screen in the app interface, allowing you to
respond without even reaching into your pocket. Nor is
it limited to texts: if you own a Bluetooth headset, you
can even channel calls through your tablet. This is one
of those apps that becomes so essential you'll wonder
how you ever coped without it.

Boomerang
Price: Free

Gmail comes as standard with all
Android devices and it's a perfectly
good way to view your mail,
but there's always room for
improvement, and that's where
Boomerang comes in. It offers all
the same functionality as the
standard Gmail app, but comes
with neat extras, such as the
ability to schedule emails for later
on, snooze incoming messages
and track responses more
effectively. It only supports Google
accounts for now, but Outlook and
Yahoo Mail are coming soon.

Skype
Price: Free

The video-calling service that all
others aim to emulate, Skype
allows you to talk face-to-face
with your friends over your 3G or
Wi-Fi connection. You can also
send instant messages and
photos using the service,
and it's even possible to call
landlines and mobiles (although
you'll need to purchase credit in
order to do so). Skype on your
tablet syncs with the web and
phone-based versions, so it's
really easy to keep all your chats
in one place.

LilyPad HD
Price: Free; Pro version available

Using instant messaging on a
tablet quickly becomes second
nature, but having to switch
between your current app and the
IM client can be a pain, especially
when you've got that massive
screen going to waste. LilyPad HD
is the solution and allows you to
chat in a window that floats over
your current app, very much like a
lily pad. It supports multiple
instant messenger clients –
including Google Hangouts, MSN
and Facebook Messenger – and is
highly customisable.

Feedly
Price: Free

When Google shut down its
popular Reader RSS service,
Feedly was the first choice of
many seeking a replacement. It's
clean, fast and intuitive to use,
and alters its presentation
depending on what size screen
you're using. Like Flipboard, it
mixes in social feeds and high-res
images, but offers a quicker,
neater experience that makes it
ideal for those moments when
you're pushed for time but want
to soak up all the latest info from
your favourite sites.

Flipboard

Price: Free

Once upon a time, dull text-only RSS readers were your only way of seeing information from all of your favourite sites in one place, but now apps like Flipboard have made things a little more dynamic and exciting. Best described as a digital magazine, Flipboard turns websites into image-rich pages that can be flicked through like a proper physical publication, and it's even possible to add social feeds such as Twitter and Instagram into the mix. It's not just about static content, either: YouTube videos can also be viewed from within the app. This is the perfect companion for those who follow a lot of sites.

ChatON

Price: Free

Samsung's instant messaging service has grown in proportion with sales of its handsets, and ChatON now rivals the likes of BBM and Google Hangouts, largely because it comes with cross-platform support, so ChatON members can communicate with each other across Android, iOS and the web. Auto translation and group chats sweeten the deal further, making this a strong choice if you're looking to keep in touch with friends online.

just.me

Price: Free

You might assume that apps such as Vine and Instagram have the monopoly on sharing images and video online, but newcomer just. me gained a lot of momentum in 2013. It now counts Miley Cyrus as one of its 300,000 users! You can share content privately with selected friends or post to the public stream, which anyone with an account can view. It's very much a work in progress, but just.me is certainly going places and could be the next big social networking success story.

Dolphin Browser

Price: Free

Ranked as the number one browser on the Google Play market with a whopping 80 million downloads, you could say that Dolphin's quality is proven by its popularity. Packed with cool features – such as customised homescreens, specialised themes, gesture control and a vast array of plugins – the browser even has its own app store. Chrome may be Android's default browser, but Dolphin has a lot more to offer.

Vine

Price: Free

Sharing static images is so last year: everyone is exchanging short video clips online these days, and Vine is at the head of the pack. The interface is clean and attractive, and close connectivity with the likes of Twitter means you can share with friends who aren't already on the fledgling social network. It might not make you a talent on the level of Spielberg, but sharing funny clips is an entertaining way to pass the time.

In this chapter

ANDROID FOR TABLETS
BEYOND THE BASICS

We uncover some of the more unusual tasks your Android tablet is capable of. Over the next few pages, you'll discover how to turn your tablet into a productivity tool, a programmable device and even a giant satnav. We've also rounded up the best office apps and utilities on the Android Market.

USING THE CALENDAR *Android's powerful Calendar app will help keep you on top of your schedule, whether at work or play. Here we reveal some of its cleverest features and explain how to take full advantage*

[Calendar screenshot showing September 2013 in Month view]

Android 4's calendar app is simple to use but deceptively powerful, allowing you to display appointments from multiple accounts side by side in the same view.

TIP
Tap the names on the right of the Calendar to make related appointments appear and disappear from the view.

So far, we've concentrated on the lighter side of life: how your Android tablet can be used for personal entertainment and keeping on top of your social life. But a tablet can be used for work, too.

At the heart of any working day is your diary. Without it, a chaos of missed meetings and forgotten events would ensue. Android 4's Calendar app is the perfect way of organising it all. You'll find it in the App Launcher.

You can choose a day, week or month view; just tap the options in the top-left of the screen to switch between them. You can navigate between days and weeks with a sideways swipe of a finger, or use the month panel on the right to skip into the future.

To add an appointment, hit the button and fill in a form. You can search appointments by keyword, set

reminders and specify if a meeting repeats daily, weekly, monthly or annually. You can also invite contacts on your tablet to meetings.

Perhaps the app's most powerful feature is its ability to synchronise appointments with the cloud; that is, all those services that live online. As with the other core apps – email and contacts – the Calendar app is linked directly to your Google account and the online Google Calendar tool.

THAT SYNCING FEELING

Set up an appointment or meeting on your tablet and it appears in your online calendar. Set one up online and your tablet will remind you it's about to start, wherever you are. Google calendars can be shared between colleagues, too, enabling you to set up appointments for a whole department to see.

The Android 4 Calendar app will even handle multiple accounts. Add another Gmail account or a corporate email account via the Accounts section in the main Settings menu, and you'll see the name of that account appear in a list, with your original Gmail account name on the right-hand side of the main calendar screen.

By default, the Calendar app will display appointments from each account side by side, colour coding appointments depending on the account from which they originated. That's brilliant, but if you're particularly busy, things can start to get messy and difficult to read. A simple tap of the finger on the account name on the right will fix that, effectively turning off appointments from that particular account, allowing you to concentrate on one schedule at a time.

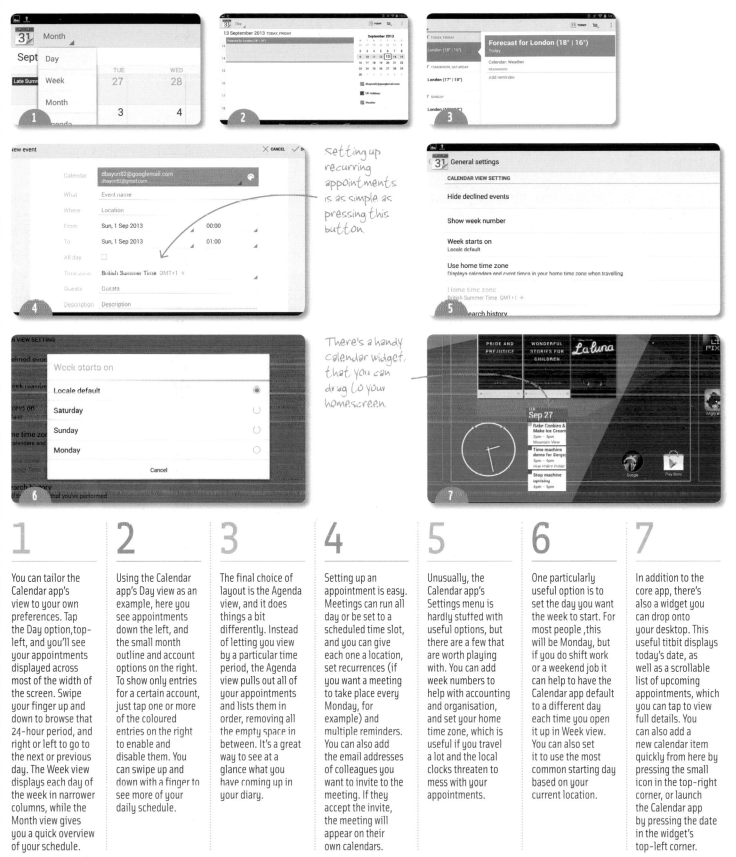

Setting up recurring appointments is as simple as pressing this button.

There's a handy calendar widget that you can drag to your homescreen.

1

You can tailor the Calendar app's view to your own preferences. Tap the Day option, top-left, and you'll see your appointments displayed across most of the width of the screen. Swipe your finger up and down to browse that 24-hour period, and right or left to go to the next or previous day. The Week view displays each day of the week in narrower columns, while the Month view gives you a quick overview of your schedule.

2

Using the Calendar app's Day view as an example, here you see appointments down the left, and the small month outline and account options on the right. To show only entries for a certain account, just tap one or more of the coloured entries on the right to enable and disable them. You can swipe up and down with a finger to see more of your daily schedule.

3

The final choice of layout is the Agenda view, and it does things a bit differently. Instead of letting you view by a particular time period, the Agenda view pulls out all of your appointments and lists them in order, removing all the empty space in between. It's a great way to see at a glance what you have coming up in your diary.

4

Setting up an appointment is easy. Meetings can run all day or be set to a scheduled time slot, and you can give each one a location, set recurrences (if you want a meeting to take place every Monday, for example) and multiple reminders. You can also add the email addresses of colleagues you want to invite to the meeting. If they accept the invite, the meeting will appear on their own calendars.

5

Unusually, the Calendar app's Settings menu is hardly stuffed with useful options, but there are a few that are worth playing with. You can add week numbers to help with accounting and organisation, and set your home time zone, which is useful if you travel a lot and the local clocks threaten to mess with your appointments.

6

One particularly useful option is to set the day you want the week to start. For most people, this will be Monday, but if you do shift work or a weekend job it can help to have the Calendar app default to a different day each time you open it up in Week view. You can also set it to use the most common starting day based on your current location.

7

In addition to the core app, there's also a widget you can drop onto your desktop. This useful titbit displays today's date, as well as a scrollable list of upcoming appointments, which you can tap to view full details. You can also add a new calendar item quickly from here by pressing the small icon in the top-right corner, or launch the Calendar app by pressing the date in the widget's top-left corner.

ESSENTIAL APPS *for productivity*

It may be a lot of fun to use, but your Android tablet also excels at the more mundane tasks in life. All you need are a few choice apps from the Market

Wunderlist
Price: **Free**

To-do lists are an essential part of many people's lives and allow us to make sense of the chaos. Wunderlist takes this concept well beyond the traditional pad and paper, offering the chance to not only create your own rundown of tasks, but also share and collaborate with other users. This is a handy feature whether you're working as part of a large team or simply want to arrange an event with close friends. The option to add media, such as photos and sounds, makes Wunderlist even more attractive for those with a busy schedule.

OfficeSuite Pro 7
Price: £9.65; trial version available

It's genuinely amazing what tablets are capable of and, with OfficeSuite Pro 7, you can effectively transform your humble device into a fully functioning office PC. It's capable of opening a broad range of documents – from text documents to spreadsheets – and can connect to cloud services such as Dropbox, Google Drive and Box for cross-platform access. It's pricey when compared to other apps, but its usefulness can't be understated.

Tabliefied Market
Price: **Free**

Tracking down apps for tablet devices isn't always easy, as Google doesn't divide up the Google Play market effectively, but Tablified Market is here to save you time and effort. It lists tablet-optimised downloads in easy-to-browse categories, but you don't have to sign in with different credit card details in order to download them: tapping each entry drops you back onto the standard Google Play storefront. A time-saving must-have for tablet owners.

CamScanner HD
Price: **Free**

Not everyone has access to a scanner or fax machine, so thank goodness for CamScanner HD, which allows you to turn pretty much anything into a PDF file that can be emailed or shared with others. It's an indispensable download if you need to keep track of receipts or submit signed documents without the use of a fax. It also makes it easy to keep track of things you've scanned, making this ideal for keeping track of business documents and other important items.

Springpad
Price: **Free**

With so many apps and websites at your fingertips, it sometimes becomes difficult to manage information, but Springpad helps by intelligently linking data. You can save web pages for viewing later, create a list of your favourite recipes or pick out your must-see movies, and get notifications when they appear on Netflix. By sorting things into folders, it's possible to pull all of the relevant information into one place. You can share folders with others users, too.

CloudMagic
Price: Free

Ever wanted to find an email or document but struggle to remember where you've put it? It's becoming a more common problem for tablet users as we become reliant on online services for data storage. CloudMagic is the tool for you: it allows you to search cloud-based services such as Gmail, Evernote, SkyDrive and Dropbox in a single query, potentially saving you hours of fruitless searching. The catch is that the more you use it the more likely you'll want to pay a monthly fee for unlimited searches, but with 50 free searches a month it's a great app, and for such a time-saving service it's money well spent.

Sticky Notes HD
Price: £1.22; free version available

The humble Post-it note is the cornerstone of many an office, and now it's possible to transfer the same concept to your tablet screen. The notes work like a widget on your homescreen and can be filled in using your finger as a pen. It's possible to use different colours for each note, allowing you to categorise your doodles. Sticky Notes has all the convenience of Post-its without the chance of them getting lost down the back of the fridge.

Google Analytics
Price: Free

If you run a website then you'll know how important it is to keep on top of traffic, social linking and the amount of time people spend reading your content, all of which can be ascertained with Google Analytics. In fact, it goes into greater detail than you might think possible, tracking what social networks are supplying your traffic and how many users are viewing your site at any one time. You can also create reports and alerts for certain events.

Jiffy
Price: Free

Time is money – or so the saying goes – and keeping track of what time you've spent on a task at work is often easier said than done. Via its stopwatch-like function, Jiffy is able to give you an overview of how much time you've expended on a particular project, thereby enabling you to manage your time better, spot areas of improvement or simply add up the total cost in terms of man-hours. It's an attractive and intuitive application, which certainly helps.

Greenlist
Price: Free

Supermarkets love to dupe us into buying things we don't need, and one way of avoiding this trap is to create an effective shopping list and stick to it. Greenlist gives you the chance to create lists manually or select recipes that generate a series of required items. By filling in details, such as cost per item, you can build up an effective shopping strategy that will ensure you only buy what you need rather than what your favoured supermarket chain wants you to purchase.

EXTENDING YOUR TABLET

If you want to use your tablet for work as well as play, you'll need to think about buying an extra accessory or two along with the apps to make the most of your device

TIP
If you buy a USB OTG (on-the-go) adapter, you may be able to use wired peripherals as well as Bluetooth ones.

We've already seen how you can use your tablet to organise your life, and that, with the addition of a few key apps, you can even produce and edit full-blown office documents. But if you really want to make the switch from laptop to tablet for working effectively on the move, you'll need to think of investing in an extra or two.

The best enhancement for any mobile worker is a proper keyboard. You can get affordable Bluetooth models from a range of manufacturers – see how to pair them in the walkthrough – while some tablets come with an optional keyboard dock to effectively turn them into a full Android laptop. Some docks include an extra battery, too, which helps to turn them into a real all-day workhorse device. The only real

drawbacks are the extra cost of adding these accessories and the additional weight in your bag.

Another option is to make use of an optional tablet stand, to neatly prop up your tablet in front of you on a desk. Some stands are designed to work with any tablet; others are specific to certain models and also charge the device; still others are incorporated into cases that also protect the tablet on the move. Whichever you prefer, they do one core job: they turn a portable device into a more fixed display.

Don't stop there. Pair a stand with a Bluetooth keyboard and mouse, and you've got yourself a neat little travelling workstation, although if you find yourself getting too carried away with accessories you might be better off just buying a laptop.

THE POWER OF THE PEN

There's another extra that can enhance the way you use your tablet: a stylus. These pen-like accessories have a rubber nib on the end that reacts to the tablet's capacitive touchscreen, allowing you to write onto the glass as if it were paper.

The Samsung Galaxy Note 8 (see p108) was designed from the outset to work with a stylus, so it includes handwriting applications and other useful tools to make the most of it. Get proficient with your stylus and you can save a huge amount of time, not to mention getting to those tiny links on web pages with more accuracy.

To help you get the most from your tablet, we've rounded up a selection of pens, keyboards, cases and other accessories in Chapter 5.

The ultimate tablet accessory is a specially designed keyboard dock, which includes an extra battery.

use the "search for devices" button to refresh the list if your keyboard isn't on there..

Some Bluetooth keyboards come with a button you can press to put it into pairing mode.

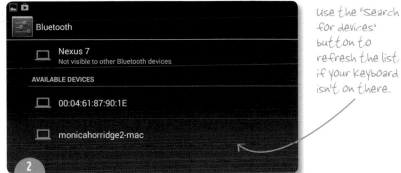

If your keyboard shows up as not connected, tap on screen once to connect it.

Make sure you enter the four-digit code on your Bluetooth keyboard quickly.

1

If you aren't already there, go to the Android desktop and drag down the Quick Settings area in the top-right corner of the screen. When the menu pops up, tap the Bluetooth button to go to the particular settings page we'll need.

2

If it isn't already on, tap the Toggle button at the top of the menu screen to enable Bluetooth. This will let the tablet start looking for nearby Bluetooth devices, including your keyboard.

3

Now switch on your Bluetooth keyboard and put it into pairing mode. This procedure varies depending on the device you're using. Our keyboard has a small button on the rear you need to press to put it into pairing mode. Normally, you'll see an LED flashing at this stage.

4

If it's not already searching, tap the "Search for devices" button back on your tablet's Settings menu, and you'll see more devices beginning to appear in the list, depending on how many are nearby. Have patience and wait for the scan to complete; your keyboard should appear near the top of the list and you'll be able to tell it apart from any computers by its icon.

5

Our test device appears as Freedom ICX Keyboard here, but that may not be the case on your device. Sometimes you'll see the product name or even just a series of letters and numbers. Whatever the naming conventions, select the device by tapping it once.

6

Next, depending on your tablet and keyboard, you may see a box appear entitled "Bluetooth pairing request". It will ask you to enter a short, four-digit code on your Bluetooth keyboard and then press Enter. Do this straightaway – if you're not quick enough off the mark, the box will disappear. The rest of the pairing procedure should complete automatically.

7

You should now be ready to start typing, but before you exit the Settings menu you can tap your paired keyboard in the list to get some more options.

TETHERING YOUR SMARTPHONE

These days, we expect an internet connection wherever we are. If you don't have a 3G-enabled tablet, you might be able to use your phone's data connection

Every modern tablet supports Wi-Fi. This means it's possible to hook up to your smartphone and share its 3G/4G connection.

Most modern smartphones have the ability to create their own private wireless hotspot.

TIP

Watch your data usage when tethering! It can quickly eat into your mobile data allowance.

W e're used to being always connected in today's world, constantly checking up on emails and social networks on our smartphones, but most tablets are still restricted to Wi-Fi, which means they're not much use for browsing when you're away from home or the office.

There is another way, though. You can set up your Android tablet to piggyback on your smartphone's data connection, allowing you to get online from anywhere with a mobile signal.

This is often called "tethering", and it can be enabled using a cable or, more conveniently, by connecting the devices together via Bluetooth or Wi-Fi. Bluetooth has a relatively short range, but as you'll have your phone on you while you use your tablet it's fine for this purpose. Your speeds will depend on whether you have 3G or 4G on your

phone, and how good the signal is, but if you find browsing on the phone an okay experience, the tablet will be no different.

Tethering can be useful for everyone at times, but it's particularly great for mobile workers and regular travellers, who can quickly get online anywhere without having to lug a laptop around in their bag.

DATA PERILS

There's one big warning to heed if you're considering the tethering route: watch your data tariffs! The situation is much better today than it was a few years ago, when most networks explicitly prohibited tethering in your contract. Now many allow it, or at least offer it as a paid-for extra to your package. Either way, you still need to be mindful of your data usage.

Every web page you browse and every app you download onto your tablet will be eating into your smartphone's data allowance, so if you have a monthly data limit in your contract, you now have two devices rapidly pushing you towards it.

The exact method will vary by phone, but it's worth using the data section of your Settings menu or a third-party data-tracking app to keep on top of things. Or you can log into your account on your mobile network's website, where you can often see a live running total throughout the month. If your network supports alerts, set them up.

The walkthrough opposite covers the setup method on the iPhone, but the process should be similar on other phones. Just look for an option for tethering, mobile hotspot or personal hotspot in the settings.

1

If you don't have a 3G-enabled tablet, you can still connect to the internet while you're out and about with Bluetooth tethering. Here's how to do it with an iPhone. First, turn on Bluetooth on your tablet. To do this, drag down from the top-right corner of the screen to bring up the Quick Settings, then tap the Bluetooth icon.

2

You can also access your connection options at any time by entering the full Settings menu and looking at the Wireless & Network segment. You can quickly enable and disable Wi-Fi and Bluetooth here, and check your data usage.

3

Just to be on the safe side, tap the Bluetooth option, turn it on, then wait as the list of nearby devices is populated. When you see your own device (it should be right at the top of the list), tap it to enable its visibility to other devices. You'll see a countdown appear on the device, as this setting is only temporary, for security and to preserve battery.

4

You need to turn on Bluetooth on your phone before you can connect. In the iPhone Settings menu, under General, select the Bluetooth option, flip the switch and go to the next step.

The settings screen is the control centre for your tablet. Any settings that can be changed are located here.

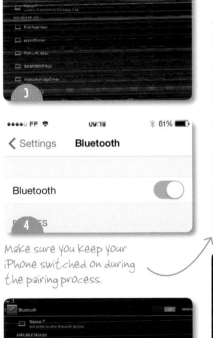

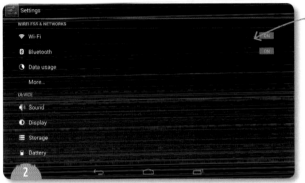

Make sure you keep your iPhone switched on during the pairing process.

5

Now you need to set up your phone to share its 3G connection. It's a simple job – just go into the Settings menu once again and, near the top, you'll find an item called Personal Hotspot. Select it, turn it on and, when the option to use Bluetooth is offered in a pop-up box, tap it.

6

Back on your tablet, after a few seconds of scanning, the iPhone should appear in the list of nearby devices. If you're having trouble, press the "Search for devices" button at the top of the screen to try again. Make sure your iPhone remains switched on.

7

Once the iPhone has been located by the tablet, select it and wait. After a few seconds, a small box should appear containing instructions on how to hook the two devices together. Ignore those and quickly, before the boxes disappear, press the Pair button on the screen of each device. Last of all, once the iPhone is displayed as paired on your tablet's screen, tap it to connect. You should now be able to use your phone's 3G connection to browse the web.

Be quick here. If you dither too long the box will disappear.

MAPS & NAVIGATION

When you start to use Google Maps on a tablet, you'll get a feel for its massive potential: your handheld device can drill down to the tiniest street or give you an overview of a continent. And it's rather handy at telling you where to go, too

Not long ago, an atlas was an essential part of any household's private library. But just like the poor old encyclopaedia, the internet has consigned atlases to the dustbin of history. Nowadays, Google Maps rules the world of cartography, and you'll be delighted to discover that one of Android 4's core apps is designed specifically to take advantage of it. As always, you'll find it in the app drawer, under the title Maps.

A tablet brings the digital world of Google Maps to life in a way that a laptop or PC just can't. Pushing and dragging the map around with your finger is effortless, and you can also pinch your fingers to zoom in and out, just as you would in the browser.

It's a beautifully designed piece of software and, as with browser-based versions of Google Maps, you can search locations and points of interest by entering a keyword. With everything from local businesses to major sightseeing attractions and hotels in Google's vast databases, you'll almost certainly find what you're looking for.

VIEW FROM ABOVE

As with Google Maps online, you can also view maps in a number of different ways. There's the standard road map view – useful for sorting out directions – but you can also display the map as a giant satellite photograph, with uncannily detailed aerial shots of (almost) everywhere on the planet. You'll find this option if you tap the maps icon in the top-left corner of the screen to reveal the options pane. It also has layers for traffic, public transport routes and cycling lanes.

That's not all, though: Google Maps can also give you walking, driving, cycling and public transport directions. Enter a destination using the keyword search then, when you've found what you're looking for, tap the car icon next to it to bring up the journey planner. Choose your mode of transport, and Maps will give you several routes, along with the expected journey time.

It gets better. Just pick a route of car directions, then tap the Start button to turn your tablet (as long as it has a GPS chip) into a full driving satnav, just like TomTom. Just watch out for your data usage. Google Maps may give you the feeling that you have the whole world at your fingertips, but in fact your tablet is downloading the maps and data, which can mount up quickly.

> ## TIP
> With two fingers resting on the map, drag them down; the map will tilt, giving a neat perspective view.

University of Westminster   BT Tower   Grange Langham Court...   All Saints Church Margar...   Rebecca Hossack Art...   Curwen & N

Google Maps lets you use your tablet just like an atlas, but if you want a real atlas you can always open Google Earth from within any map.

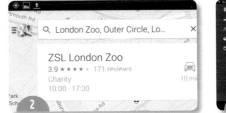

You can achieve a lot with the basic map view, but tap the icon in the top-left to get more views.

Traffic indicators will help you plan your journeys more wisely.

1

Launch the Google Maps app from either the desktop shortcut or the app drawer. There's so much it can do. The basic map view is your starting point, and it displays accurate street and landmark information, along with stations, parks and rivers. You can work entirely in this mode if it's easiest, although you're missing out on much of the power of Google Maps if you do.

2

Enter a destination in the search bar at the top of the screen to jump to a new location. This being Google, several other services are linked into the results, so you can see information such as user reviews and opening times without leaving the map. To bring the map back to your current location, tap the compass in the bottom-right corner; tap it again to zoom into a closer, angled view that faces the same way you are.

3

Tap the Maps icon in the top-left corner to pull out the options pane. This is where you can change from the basic map view to more powerful alternatives. Add traffic information onto roads; include public transport and cycling routes on the map; change to an accurate satellite view to see exactly what's in each location; or even open the location in Google Earth, the 3D mapping tool.

4

You can combine multiple map overlays for better effect. Here, we've switched to the satellite view to get a better visual idea of our destination, then overlaid the traffic information on top of the roads so we can see any black spots that would be best avoided. The blue dot is you, and it will follow the roads as you move around.

5

If you want to make things really useful, switch to satellite view, then tap the compass icon in the bottom-right corner twice. The map will spin around to match your current orientation, then dive down into a semi-3D view. It's a great way to navigate while out walking.

6

Navigation is a huge part of Maps. Tap the split arrow icon on the search bar, and you can enter a start and end location for a route. The top of the bar will now have car, public transport, bike and walking icons, and you can switch between them to see how your route changes live on the map. Several routes may be offered and, if you choose the ideal one and tap the Start button that appears, you'll get full satnav directions.

7

Google Earth is the final piece of the Maps puzzle and, although it's technically a separate app that opens up alongside Maps, it's still a stunning tool. Okay, it might not be as useful on a daily basis as a map of your area, but there's no denying exploring the sights of a city looks much better in full 3D.

MAXIMISE YOUR BATTERY LIFE

With so many features on tap, if you're not careful your tablet will soon have its battery life sucked out of it. Here we explain the chief culprits and offer some tips on how to conserve power on the move

---

Battery   ⟳ REFRESH

52% - Charging (USB)

21m 29s on battery

☼	Screen	16%
	Media server	15%
	Android System	14%
	Android OS	11%
	mm-qcamera-daemon	8%

If you want to see exactly which apps and components have been using your battery, and for how long, check out the battery usage page. You'll find this in the Settings menu under Device.

The best tablets will last for more than ten hours of continuous use from a single charge, and for several days if used more sporadically. If you're not careful, however, you may find yourself having to charge your tablet more often than you'd like. There's nothing more irritating than taking your tablet from its bag to be told the battery is running low.

If you follow a few simple guidelines, however, you should be able to keep going as long as the Duracell bunny. The place to start is the screen. Go to the Settings menu and scroll down to the Device section where you'll find Battery. This excellent screen shows you which apps and components are taxing your battery most. The screen will probably be top of this list: it's the most power-hungry component of your tablet.

If you want your tablet to last longer between charges, you need to minimise the screen's power draw, and there are several ways of doing this. The key is to make sure it isn't on for any longer than necessary and, when it is on, to keep the brightness as low as possible.

DATA DRAW

The other key things to consider are the mobile broadband and Wi-Fi adapters your tablet uses to connect to the internet. With browsing at the core of what you do with your tablet, it's little wonder these give the battery a thorough workout. And with so many apps constantly checking for messages and updates in the background, things can quickly get out of hand.

You can find details opposite on what to do to minimise the impact internet connectivity has on your battery, but,

again, the key is control. In the Sync section of the Settings menu, you can change when and how often your tablet synchronises your various email and social networking accounts.

Other apps – such as weather updates, a widget that checks stocks or a newsfeed reader – may also be listed here. Ask yourself if you really need this information to be updated constantly. If the answer is no, change the settings of each app individually to make sure they aren't sneaking onto the internet behind your back.

Last, but by no means least, take a trip to the Settings menu of the Google Play Store and make sure that automatic updates for all your apps are switched off. App updates can be quite large, and updates, especially over a mobile internet connection, can be a serious drain on your battery.

TIP

Keeping on top of battery-hoggers can be tiresome, but battery-saving apps on the Android Market will help.

WALKTHROUGH *Seven steps to better battery life*

You can see how much data every element of your tablet is using in the Settings menu.

Not all apps with internet connectivity will be listed here. Make sure you know what they are and check their settings individually.

1

The screen on your tablet is the main culprit when it comes to swallowing up battery life. The brighter it is and the longer it's on, the more power it uses. You can see how much of your battery is being used by the screen in the Battery section of the tablet's Settings menu. There will also be a shortcut to the display settings where you can do something about it.

2

Pull down the settings bar (the top-right of the screen) and tap the Brightness button to bring up the slider. Drag this to the left to dim the screen – you can probably still comfortably use your tablet at lower than the default level – or tap the Auto button to use your tablet's ambient light sensor to raise and lower the brightness to suit your location.

3

That pull-down settings bar also has a couple of other tools to reduce battery consumption. Tap the Aeroplane Mode button to disable all of your tablet's power-hogging data connections, such as Wi-Fi and Bluetooth. Also, turn off the Auto-Rotate function to save a bit more juice – albeit not much – from all those portrait to landscape switches.

Google apps location settings

Let Google apps access your location

A couple of things to note:

- Google apps may access your location while you're not using them.
- This setting affects Google apps only. To turn off location access by non-Google apps, go to **Settings access.**

Location access

4

Another way of rationing your tablet's use of its 3G and Wi-Fi connectivity is to alter its Sync settings. Under Sync in the Settings menu, you'll see several options for managing the frequency with which the tablet and specific apps connect to the internet. Disable background data, and apps will connect to the internet only when you ask them to.

5

Location data is another reason for a dramatically declining battery, and sometimes you won't even realise it's happening. At times when you need the extra juice, switch off location access for all apps and services. It's in the Settings menu, under Location Access, and also in the settings menus of several Google apps, such as Maps.

6

Some apps may be set to automatically download and install updates without your intervention. To stop this and save battery life, go to the Google Play Store, tap the Settings button in the top-right of the screen and tap "Auto-update apps" to bring up the option. Change it to "Do not auto-update apps" to give yourself more control over your data use.

7

For ultimate control over battery-hogging apps and hardware, download a battery management app from the Google Play Store. JuiceDefender is our favourite. It lets you manage power-related settings on an app-by-app basis, allowing Gmail access to the net, for instance, but stopping TweetComb from downloading updates until you launch the app itself.

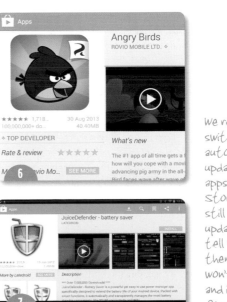

We recommend switching off automatic updating for apps. The Play Store app will still check for updates and tell you about them, but it won't download and install them for you.

PROGRAMMING YOUR TABLET

As if Android tablets weren't flexible enough already, you can make them even better. The magic of Tasker lets you create your very own Android apps without learning a programming language

Think of anything you want to do with your tablet, and chances are there will be an app in the Android Market that lets you do it. But what if you want to do something that isn't covered? What if, no matter how much digging around you do, you just can't find an app to do what you want?

If that's the case, and if you're of a technical bent, you might want to investigate Tasker. It isn't free, but it enables you to program your tablet to do almost anything you can think of without the need to learn a programming language. Want to send an email to your other half when you reach a certain stage of your commute? Set the tablet to silent when you go to bed? With Tasker, you can do all this and more.

The key to working with Tasker is to understand Profiles, Contexts and Actions, the three core elements that Tasker uses to do its job. Profiles are the tasks or individual jobs you want Tasker to carry out: sending an email based on your location, for instance, or adjusting the volume level whenever your plug in a pair of headphones. You can create any number of Profiles, and each can be switched on or off, as you see fit.

PUTTING IT IN CONTEXT

That's easy to wrap your head around, but now we get to the more difficult part: Contexts. In Tasker, each profile has one Context attached to it, and this acts as the trigger that sets the Profile in motion. This can be almost anything you can think of. You can use hardware triggers: onscreen gestures, plugging in those headphones or reaching a certain battery level, for example.

There are location-based Contexts that trigger actions depending on where you are. Apps can be triggers, too, setting off actions when they're launched, or you can use the time or date and even certain system-level events. You can trigger your Profile every time you turn on or shut down your tablet, for example.

Finally, Actions are what you want your tablet to do once the Profile is activated. In the walkthrough, we explain how to set up a Profile that launches the Music app, sets the volume level to ten, then tells you what it's done in a pop-up message, but you can add many more actions.

In fact, with a little perseverance and application, you can do almost anything you want with Tasker. The only limit is your imagination.

> **TIP**
> If you don't want to splash your cash, there's a 14-day free trial of Tasker available on the Android Market.

Tasker lets you set up any number of different automated tasks, and they're easy to switch on and off at will.

We've picked a hardware action to trigger our program, but you can base your programs on location, time or gesture.

1

Before you do anything else, set up a new action, or Profile as Tasker calls them. We're going to create a profile that sets the music volume to ten and automatically launches the Music app whenever headphones are plugged in. To create a new profile, tap the plus symbol at the bottom of the screen.

2

Now you need to select your Profile's first context. Despite the obscure name, a context is simply a trigger, like the movement sensor that sets off a burglar alarm. In our case, the trigger is a pair of headphones being plugged in, but it could be the time of day or the launching of a specific app. Tap State, Hardware, Headset Plugged, then tap the Tasker icon in the top-left corner of the screen.

3

Next, we need to tell Tasker what to do when the headphones have been plugged in and the context has been triggered. Tap the New Task button and type a name for the action in the box: we're going to set the volume and launch the Music app, so we've called it Setvol Launchmusic. Tap the tick and you'll be presented with the Task Edit box; this is where you define the actions that make up the task.

We're using the Play Music app, but you can use any app you want to trigger a Tasker action.

4

We're going to tell the tablet to set its volume to medium. Tap the '+' symbol at the bottom of the Task Edit window, then select Audio, Media Volume and adjust the slider to the appropriate level. Drag it to the right a few steps, then tap the Tasker icon in the top-left corner. You'll now be returned to the Task Edit box, where the new task will appear at the top of the list.

5

To launch the Music app, we need to create another stage. Tap the '+' symbol in the Task Edit window once again, then select the App option in the following window, tap Load App and select Play Music from the scrolling grid of applications. To finish, tap the Tasker icon in the top-left corner and you should now see another action added to the Task Edit window.

6

As a finishing touch, we're going to generate a pop-up box as a reminder that the volume level has been changed. Once again, the process is simple: tap the plus symbol at bottom of the screen, but this time select the Alert option, followed by Popup. On the next screen, type "The volume level has been set to 10" into the Text box and tap the Tasker icon in the top-left corner to confirm.

7

All that remains is to make sure the Profile is up and running. Tap the Tasker icon in the top-left corner and, on the following screen, ensure the switch next to your profile is set to on, then quit out of Tasker using your browser's back button. Now, whenever you plug in your headphones, the tablet will automatically launch the Music app and set the volume to ten.

PHOTO EDITING ON YOUR TABLET

Hidden away in Android's Gallery app is a range of powerful photo-editing tools that can help turn your humdrum snaps into eye-catching stunners

The edit view looks slightly different in landscape view, with options and thumbnails appearing to the right instead of below your photo.

TIP
If you're not happy with an edit, don't worry you can reverse your changes using the Undo button.

The quality of the screen on the best Android tablets makes them ideal for viewing photos. But once you've seen what you thought were great shots on the screen of a Sony Xperia Tablet Z, you might wish you were a better photographer!

Never fear: with a little judicious editing, those flat, dull photos can be turned into something you'd be proud to print out and mount in a picture frame. And you probably won't be surprised to discover that your Android tablet has all the tools you need.

If you're not editing photos taken by the tablet itself, the first step will be to get the photos from your smartphone or camera onto your tablet. The most straightforward way to do this may be simply to connect both tablet and camera to your laptop and copy the files across manually.

If you're feeling more adventurous, you could bypass involving another computer completely. The most convenient method for photo transfer is to use a cloud service such as Google+ or Dropbox to which you save your photos. You can then download the images to your tablet ready for editing. Alternatively, buy a USB On-the-Go adapter and you'll be able to copy files across by plugging in your camera, memory card or smartphone directly to your tablet's USB port.

READY FOR EDITING

Once you've transferred your images, you can use your tablet's Gallery app to make adjustments. Launch it from the app drawer, find and open the image, then launch the photo-editing mode by tapping the pencil icon in the bottom-left corner (this might be represented by three intersecting circles on some tablets).

Once you're in, tweaks are divided into four categories: filters, frames, cropping and straightening, and brightness and contrast. Filters can give your pictures a vintage look; frames provides a variety of realistic-looking outlines for your photo; cropping can be used to reposition subjects within the photo and straighten wonky horizons; and brightness and contrast lets you correct overly dark or overly bright photos. It also includes a sharpening tool for bringing out the details, and colour adjustments to help liven up dull, washed-out snaps.

For more power, there are hundreds of suitable apps out there. Even professional snappers are catered for, with apps such as Photo Mate offering raw file compatibility and processing.

Wonky horizons are simple to correct.

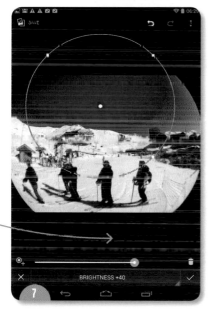

Android's range of filters is extensive.

BY cropping, you can remove distracting elements from your photos.

use selective edits to change only parts of your photo.

BRIGHTNESS +40

1

First things first, you need to choose a photo to edit. Go to your tablet's Gallery app. You'll find this in the app drawer alongside all the other apps. The first screen displays your photos in a series of Albums. Select one, then pick a photo to edit.

2

Once you've picked a photo to edit, it will appear full screen. Give the photo a quick tap, and you'll see a number of buttons and menu options appear at the top and bottom of the screen. The button we're interested in is the pencil icon in the bottom-left corner. Tap it and you'll be whisked off into editing mode.

3

On the next screen, you'll see the chosen photo with a number of different icons and thumbnail images running along the bottom of the screen. This default editing view is the filters view, which allows you to apply instant special effects to change the overall look of your photo. Tap each thumbnail in turn to see if anything takes your fancy.

4

Tapping the square icon at the bottom of the screen adds a frame to your picture. There are loads to choose from here, from a plain white border to vintage slide effects. Again, tap each in turn to see if there's anything you like and swipe left or right to see more.

5

The next icon along gives you a number of different options: you can crop in to focus on important details or to remove unwanted objects at the edges of your photo, you can straighten wonky horizons, rotate the photo, or flip the photo horizontally or vertically using the Mirror option.

6

The last icon in the row delivers more advanced editing controls – the type you're likely to see in a more advance PC image-editing app. Tap it and you'll be able to adjust settings such as exposure, contrast, sharpness, vibrancy and saturation. Local tool is one of the most useful: scroll to the right to find it and move to the next step.

7

The Local tool allows you to apply certain effects to only parts of an image. To brighten the sky in this photo, drag the circle to a central point in the sky, and re-size it using the small dots on its perimeter so the red highlighting covers the area you want to edit. Then adjust the Brightness slider at the bottom up and down until you get the effect you want.

ESSENTIAL APPS *The best tools and utilities*

Want to access your desktop PC from your tablet, touch-type on the screen or protect your device from viruses? This selection of useful utilities lets you do all that and more

ezPDF Reader
Price: £2.50

The large screens found on tablets make them ideal for reading books and magazines, but they're also great for perusing PDF documents. ezPDF Reader is a compact app that supports note-taking, text highlighting and embedded video. Unlike its rivals, it's fast and boasts a visually pleasing "page flipping" effect. All of your PDFs are laid out on a rather fetching imitation bookshelf, and the cherry on top is its text-to-speech feature, which means you can listen to your PDFs as well as read them. A "lite" version is also available to try before you buy.

File Manager HD
Price: Free

It's amazing that many Android tablets don't come with a file manager by default, but you can rectify this oversight by installing this feature-rich app. Cloud support is included, and you can even access files over FTP services. File Manager HD makes good use of HD displays, giving you full control over your device's cavernous internal memory. It's ad supported, but you can remove these by making an in-app purchase.

Wi-Fi Manager
Price: Free

Your Android tablet may be pretty good at connecting to open Wi-Fi hotspots, but there's plenty of room for improvement. WiFi Manager provides just that: it gives you a better idea of signal strength, allows you to rename access points and switch between hotspots with a single tap. This last feature is a real time-saver and means you don't have to keep dropping into the Settings menu to toggle your tablet.

TeamViewer
Price: Free

Everyone dreads getting that phone call from a friend or relative in need of tech support, because it's almost impossible to assist down a phone line, but not anymore. TeamViewer grants the power to control a PC remotely via your tablet. Built around the tablet interface, the app allows you to interact with distant computers (including your own) and share files between your device and the host PC. It's all very futuristic and incredibly useful.

Dashlane Password Manager
Price: Free

Passwords are required for practically every activity you indulge in online, and web security experts recommend you never use the same one twice. Remembering all those passwords is impossible unless you're a genius, so for everyone else there's Dashlane, an app that allows you to store multiple login details and secure them with a master password. Dashlane auto-fills password fields on sites, taking the pain out of logging in.

SwiftKey Keyboard
Price: £2.99

Android's support for custom keyboards has given rise to a flood of alternatives, and SwiftKey is surely the best. It uses a prediction engine that learns how you type and eventually becomes so adept that it can guess your next word with uncanny accuracy. Trace-to-type has been added, and if you have SwiftKey on your phone, too, you can use the cloud storage service to share the keyboard's knowledge base across multiple devices, meaning that every piece of Android tech you own can be blessed with super-fast text input.

AirDroid
Price: Free

Cloud services such as Google Drive and Dropbox may have removed the need to plug your Android tablet into your PC, but every now and then you may find yourself reaching for that USB cable in order to shift files around. AirDroid aims to zap that cable once and for all, as it allows you to manage your device over a Wi-Fi network. You can also stream video from your tablet's camera, effectively turning it into a webcam.

Google Drive
Price: Free

Google's answer to Dropbox has gone from strength to strength in the past 12 months, offering robust and deep-rooted connectivity with the Android operating system. You can store practically anything, and Drive's thumbnail views make it easy to sift through your treasured files, photos and videos. Since it's built on the foundation of Google Docs, Drive makes it easy to share and collaborate with friends and work colleagues.

LendList
Price: Free

Music CDs and DVDs may be slowly dying out, but that doesn't mean the practice of lending such items out to friends has stopped just yet. If you're the kind of person who's forever lending out your copy of *The Sopranos* to friends and forgetting who has it, then you need LendList on your tablet. You can even set reminders and loan limits (although this is unlikely to earn you any attractive nicknames), and export them to your Google Calendar.

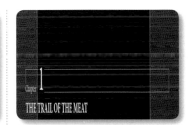

Touch Blocker
Price: Free

Touchscreens are at the heart of modern technology, but they're a little too easy to accidentally touch when you're holding your device. Touch Blocker does exactly what you'd expect from its name: you can assign "dead zones" on the tablet's screen that won't register a touch if you happen to brush your finger against them. For the clumsier among us, the reduced number of unintended touches can save lots of time and frustration.

ESSENTIAL APPS *Images and video*

From forming your own digital masterpieces, enhancing photos and shooting video, here are our favourite apps that will enable you to unleash your creative side

Autodesk SketchBook Pro for Tablets

Price: £3.35

While there are plenty of doodling tools available on tablets, Autodesk SketchBook Pro takes things to the next level with a customisable UI, 60 preset brush types and the ability to export to files that can be edited using Photoshop. It also supports a "pen only" mode for devices that come with special touchscreen pens, which increases accuracy dramatically and allows you to create some truly amazing digital masterpieces. SketchBook Pro serves as an able companion app to Photoshop Touch.

Glimmr Pro

Price: £1.62

You might assume that it's always best to go with the official option when picking apps, but Glimmr disproves this theory: it's a Flickr client that bests Flickr's own app in every way imaginable. Not only is it easier to use, it features better notifications, a homescreen widget and the ability to use high-resolution thumbnails (especially useful on tablets). The developers also have a user forum where you can suggest new features, so the app will only get better over time.

Snapseed

Price: Free

These days, taking a decent photo isn't just about pointing a camera at something attractive – there's so much more you can do in post-production to make your snap look like something David Bailey would be proud to put his name to. Snapseed is arguably the best photo-editing app available for Android tablets, allowing you to turn almost any image into a work of art: you can enhance shots and add funky filters to suit your personal taste.

MX Player

Price: Free

You might assume that your Android tablet's default media player is good enough to play back most video files, but this isn't always the case. MX Player is a powerful video app that harnesses the power of the latest processors for better playback. As well as being fast, it also comes with support for a wide range of codecs and fun features such as coloured subtitles and a mode that prevents your offspring from activating any other tablet features during playback.

InstaGrid

Price: Free

Instagram may be the first choice for snap-happy tablet users, but InstaGrid provides the same functionality, except with large-screen devices in mind. It makes sifting through your photo stream much easier and supports comment posting "liking" of snaps. The catch is that you can't post images to Instagram via this app. If you have the official app to hand, though, you can use InstaGrid in tandem for the full experience.

Adobe Photoshop Touch
Price: £6.99

Adobe's world-famous Photoshop desktop application is a market leader in image manipulation, and it's now available in tablet format. It comes with many of the same features of its PC-based relation, including the ability to work with different tools, add layers and edit large-scale images. It doesn't end there, either: If you're signed up to Adobe Creative Cloud, you can also make use of 2GB of free online storage to sync projects between your tablet and desktop, allowing you to work effortlessly while on the road and then transfer your work to your PC when you get back home.

Magisto
Price: Free

Just as mobile phones supplanted the compact digital camera for many people, tablet are now threatening the humble handycam. You can shoot HD video and edit it immediately with apps such as Magisto without even having to download to your PC. Magisto offers all the usual editing tools, as well as a powerful analyser that automatically links together clips to create decent movies, which you can then share with friends and family.

Floating Video Player
Price: 64p

If you've used a Samsung device recently then you may have noticed the brilliant "floating" video player, which allows you to watch movies while performing other tasks. If you don't own a tablet with this feature in place then don't worry: Floating Video Player offers the same functionality. You can send emails, browse the web or post on Twitter, all at the same time as enjoying a movie or an episode of your favourite TV show.

Google+
Price: Free

Google+ is Google's attempt to unseat the likes of Twitter and Facebook, but it comes with a handy feature: automatic uploading of your photos to the cloud. Once uploaded, you can view them from within your Google account (and your tablet's Gallery app), sort them into albums and share them with people online. Google+ may not have the same traction as its social networking rivals, but this feature alone makes the app an indispensable download.

Paper Camera
Price: Free

Many photo-editing tools focus on fine-tuning your shots, but Paper Camera has no such aims: it's all about making images look radically different. You can turn your shot into a pencil sketch or even apply a filter that makes it appear like a page lifted from a comic book. They may not be works of art you'll want to hang on your wall, but Paper Camera has an uncanny knack of making ordinary shots look extraordinary.

In this chapter

ANDROID FOR TABLETS
HARDWARE REVIEWS

If you haven't bought a tablet already, you'll find everything you need to make your choice in this bumper chapter. We've reviewed 13 tablets that cover the full range of prices, from bargain basement to premium iPad rivals. We've tested the tablets to within an inch of their lives and, to cap it all, we've also picked out some essential accessories, speakers and cases.

While many manufacturers are going widescreen, the Iconia A1 sticks to a more square shape.

Acer Iconia A1

An attractive price, but a poor screen and mediocre real-world performance put paid to this tablet's aspirations

Just a year or two ago we'd never have imagined we'd now have 8in tablets costing just £170. Yet that's exactly the price of the Acer Iconia A1 – a full £100 cheaper than an iPad mini.

The big question is how many compromises Acer has had to make. The Iconia A1 starts off well, with a screen resolution of 768 x 1,024 – the same as the iPad mini – and the screen feels spacious next to widescreen 7in tablets.

The quality isn't so impressive. The touchscreen layer adds grain, and the screen brightness is limited, so don't expect to see much outdoors. Colours aren't very vibrant, either.

SPECS

PRICE: £170
SCREEN: 7.9in 768 x 1,024
STORAGE: 16GB
PROCESSOR: Quad-core 1.2GHz MediaTek MT8389W
RAM: 1GB
WEIGHT: 400g
WDH: 146 x 11 x 209mm

With a quad-core 1.2GHz MediaTek processor and 1GB of RAM, it outpaced other cheap tablets in our benchmarks, and in real-world tests we found menus and web pages scrolled smoothly, but the general feel was less positive: navigating the OS felt sluggish, and apps loaded slowly. Graphics are also a weak point: the demanding Real Racing 3 dropped frames noticeably at times.

Battery life of 8hrs 3mins isn't amazing, and although the A1 does have a 5-megapixel rear-facing camera, it's fixed-focus, and our photos showed poor image quality and a lack of detail. As for the hardware, the plastic chassis

flexes when you squeeze the rear panel. A micro-HDMI socket and microSD slot do add some versatility, so you could add to the included 16GB of storage.

The one big plus point is Android 4.2.2, which brings several useful features, including multiple user profiles and lockscreen widgets. There's also a selection of Acer software preinstalled, although these apps are of less interest.

So, all in all, the Iconia A1 is something of a damp squib. While an 8in tablet for £170 might look like a steal, you're ultimately better off either paying more or sticking with a smaller-screened device in daily use.

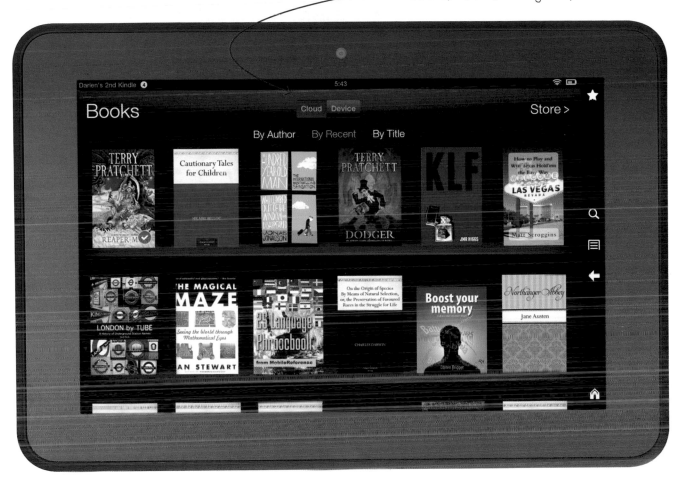

You get Amazon's own Appstore on the Kindle Fire HD, rather than Google Play.

Amazon Kindle Fire HD 8.9

The bigger of the two Kindle Fire HD tablets has a fantastic screen and built-in access to plenty of content, but it's restrictive in many ways, too

For a £70 premium over the 7in model, the Kindle Fire HD 8.9 is a more comfortable experience, with thumb-sized edges sitting neatly around its 8.9in display. And a fine display it is, with a 1,920 x 1,200 resolution that's a real step up in quality from the 7in. It has blinding brightness and excellent contrast, and it's bold and crisp – a real delight to read text on.

Predictably, watching video via Lovefilm is a pleasant experience, with excellent viewing angles and rich colours. Dual-band wireless helps ensure the streaming experience stays smooth throughout the home.

SPECS

PRICE: From £229
SCREEN: 8.9in 1,920 x 1,200
STORAGE: 16GB
PROCESSOR: Dual-core 1.5GHz Ti
RAM: 1GB
WEIGHT: 567g
WDH: 239 x 9 x 163mm

The speakers are nice and punchy, too, although if you turn up the volume they do start to distort. The glossy screen is susceptible to reflections, but a micro-HDMI port at the base makes it easy to hook the tablet up to a TV.

The battery handles entertainment well. Our video rundown test looped for 12hrs 26mins. Streaming wirelessly from Lovefilm sucks the power at a faster rate, but Amazon still promises more than ten hours of viewing time.

Through all of this, Amazon's custom front-end puts your content front and centre, so as a tablet for consuming books and videos it's effective. But if

you're looking for a more general-purpose tablet, it's less rosy. Its dual-core 1.5GHz processor slogged through our benchmarks with unremarkable results. The upcoming Amazon Kindle Fire HDX 8.9in may remedy this, with significantly faster internals, but the Amazon tie-in will remain, complete with the limited Amazon Appstore, which replaces Google Play.

All of this means you're probably better off buying a generic Android tablet and installing Netflix and the Kindle app. The Kindle Fire HD is tempting, but not for everyone.

On a Kindle Fire device, your content is joined by recommended titles from the Amazon store.

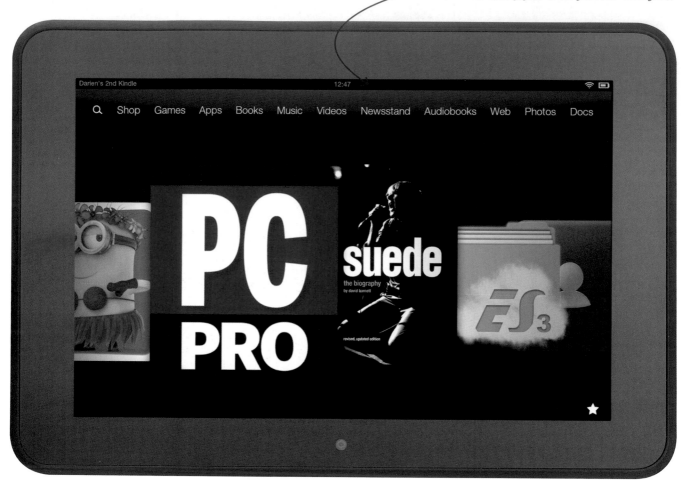

Amazon Kindle Fire HD 7

A fine tablet that's custom-built for buying books and movies, although for mainstream apps and web browsing you may want to look elsewhere

As soon as you pick up the Fire HD, it's clear this isn't just another Kindle. For one thing, it weighs a lumpen 395g – more than double the regular E Ink Kindle. It's larger, too, with a chunky, soft-plastic back, a wide bezel and a full-colour 1,280 x 800 IPS touchscreen.

True, it undercuts Google's rival Nexus 7 on price, but there's a hidden cost. Amazon's tablet uses a custom shop-front interface, making it feel like a device designed primarily for consuming content – and for buying more. As an example, the first item in the horizontal navigation menu on the

SPECS

PRICE: £159
SCREEN: 7in 800 x 1,280
STORAGE: 16GB
PROCESSOR: Dual-core 1.2GHz OMAP 4460
RAM: 1GB
WEIGHT: 395g
WDH: 137 x 10.3 x 193mm

homescreen is "Shop", and the last is "Offers". Below that comes content consumption, in the form of a carousel display of all your purchased books. As you use the tablet, recently accessed items and apps join this carousel, and when you stop on an item the smaller icons at the bottom update to show relevant links. For books, this is "customers also bought": tap on a title and you're whisked directly to the Amazon website, to complete the purchase in the built-in Silk browser.

As for reading on this tablet, text is remarkably clean and sharp, with superb contrast. In sunlight, the Fire

HD's screen jacks up to a spectacular brightness, remaining readable so long as you angle the high-gloss display to avoid reflections. The only real downer is the sheer heft of it, which makes it tiring to hold one-handed.

Amazon is also keen for you to use the Kindle Fire HD for movies and music, with the buttons and connectors positioned to imply a video-friendly landscape orientation. The speakers won't fill a room, but they sound great, with an impressively airy tone. Syncing music from your PC is simply a matter of copying files into the Kindle Fire HD's Music folder, or using Amazon's Cloud

The Fire is bigger and heavier than a standard Kindle, but it's comfortable enough to hold for long periods

A micro-HDMI socket on the bottom lets you play your downloaded movies on a TV

Player service, which automatically syncs with the device.

Video comes via Lovefilm's Instant service, from which movies and TV episodes can be downloaded or streamed, and Amazon's own store as well. A micro-HDMI socket allows you to enjoy video on the big screen.

It's only when we reach apps that the Fire HD's glow starts to fade. Predictably, the device comes with Amazon's Appstore. All the big apps are here, along with the tempting Free App of the Day, but you can't install Google Play on the Fire HD at all –it won't even run – so if you're already using an

Android smartphone or tablet your existing apps are useless here.

And what of performance? On paper, the 1.2GHz OMAP 4460 processor sounds reasonable for a small tablet, but the Kindle Fire HD is left lagging behind the newer Nexus 7, and in real-world use we found navigating the interface a distinctly jerky experience.

Amazon's heavy customisation doesn't help, seeming to prioritise its own commercial interests above yours. To access the web browser from the main menu, for example, you must scroll past seven categories of purchasable content. Wake the device

up from sleep and the lockscreen shows adverts for Amazon partners – a "feature" you're can pay £10 to disable.

As for battery life, don't expect miracles. We were able to watch 6hrs 28mins of full-screen video; if you switch off Wi-Fi, expect about an extra two-and-a-half hours on top of that.

If you like the idea of a multimedia tablet tied into one retailer, the Fire HD makes sense, but it's probably worth waiting until the Kindle Fire HDX – with its higher resolution screen – arrives before making your purchase. For everyone else, the freedom of the new Nexus 7 makes it a better long-term bet.

The ultra-cheap 80 Titanium comes with Android 4.1.1, and Archos has largely left it alone.

Archos 80 Titanium

Impressive build and slick performance go some way towards making up for this cheap tablet's disappointing battery life and awful camera

Archos has a reputation for affordability, so it's no surprise its 80 Titanium comes in at an incredible £125. But this isn't some plasticky 7in knock-off; it boasts an 8in display that's bright and colourful, and a solid chassis that feels made to last.

The only outward sign of budget-trimming is the 768 x 1,024 display. Its an IPS panel with wide viewing angles, but it's grainy and its maximum brightness is nowhere near dearer tablets. Colours and contrast are okay, though, and images look livelier than you'd expect.

The 80 Titanium's specification is middling in most respects, but works

SPECS

PRICE: £125
SCREEN: 8in 768 x 1,024
STORAGE: 8GB
PROCESSOR: Dual-core 1.6GHz ARM A9
RAM: 1GB
WEIGHT: 440g
WDH: 154 x 10 x 200mm

perfectly well in practice. That £125 gets you a dual-core 1.6GHz ARM A9 processor and 1GB of RAM, and it performed well. Rayman Jungle Run ran smoothly, and Dead Trigger and Reckless Racing 2 barely slowed down.

In everyday use, the OS felt just as slick. Archos has left Android 4.1.1 largely untouched, with only a couple of proprietary apps coming preinstalled.

On to build, the metal rear panel feels robust and looks smart, and its white bezel stands out from all the black on the shelves. It's a touch heavy at 440g, and a little thick, too, at 10mm, but this leaves room for a bevy of connections.

It has micro-USB, a mini-HDMI output and a microSD slot to add to the meagre 8GB of built-in storage. We have only one design complaint: the home button is oddly placed on the top-left edge, just above the volume rocker.

Elsewhere, there are bigger problems. The battery lasted a woeful 5hrs 10mins – three hours short of the Acer Iconia A1. There's no light sensor for automatic screen brightness, and no Bluetooth. The rear camera is so terrible we'd rather Archos hadn't bothered.

It's no all-rounder, then, but it does at least get the basics right. If you're on a shoestring budget that may be enough.

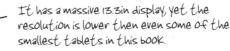
It has a massive 13.3in display, yet the resolution is lower then even some of the smallest tablets in this book.

Archos FamilyPad 2

Astonishingly big, heavy and awkward to hold, let alone use. With slow performance and a poor screen, we'd steer well clear

For sensible reasons, larger screens have mainly been for laptop-tablet hybrid devices, with tablets sticking to 10in and below. In case you can't tell from the photo on this page, the Archos FamilyPad 2 throws that logic out of the window.

With a 13.3in screen diagonal, it's absolutely huge: a massive 337mm wide, 230mm tall and 11.6mm deep. And, with a weight of 1.3kg, it's as heavy as the latest sleek Ultrabook laptops. Such size has its major advantages. On the right-hand edge, you'll find the power socket, plus mini-HDMI, a 3.5mm headset jack, a microSD expansion slot

SPECS

PRICE: £250
SCREEN: 13.3in 1,280 x 800
STORAGE: 8GB
PROCESSOR: Dual-core 1.6GHz ARM A9
RAM: 1GB
WEIGHT: 1.3kg
WDH: 337 x 11.6 x 230mm

to add to the built-in 8GB of storage, and a pair of micro-USB ports. One of those is for charging and transferring data; the other is for connecting external storage devices via an adapter cable that, alas, isn't included.

But still, that size! It's far too heavy to use one-handed, and if you were hoping the up-side would be the inclusion of the best screen available on tablets today, you're in for a disappointment. The FamilyPad has a paltry 800 x 1,280 resolution stretched across that 13.3in diagonal, so it's less sharp than any other tablet in this book. This gives the picture a grainy, old-school look, and

poor vertical viewing angles mean it can be unreadable if you lay it flat on your lap. The contrast is very low and the maximum brightness is even worse; don't take this tablet outdoors.

Still, with fewer pixels, surely it would perform well? Alas not, with keyboard lag epitomising a sluggish all-round feel, and benchmark results that put it at the foot of all performance tables.

It's an odd product whichever way you look at it. £250 for a massive device looks like good value, but we'd prefer any of the smaller tablets here over this slow, impractical monster. Such a large tablet makes no logical sense.

The Archos 101 XS comes with a bundled keyboard dock, turning it into a neat little 10in workstation.

Archos 101 XS

A decent price for a 10in tablet with a bundled keyboard dock, but the cheap build quality and below average performance count this tablet out

Archos' speciality these days is the production of budget Android tablets, and the Archos 101 XS – part of its Gen10 XS Series – is well priced for a 10.1in tablet.

You get plenty for your money, as the tablet comes with a keyboard cover in the box. When you need to do some typing, it docks neatly into this, with a small plastic arm to prop it up. When you're done, the cover snaps magnetically onto the front of the tablet, neatly protecting the screen. It's an elegant-looking solution.

However, when it comes to build quality, the 101 XS fails to impress. It's

SPECS

PRICE: £233
SCREEN: 10.1in 1,280 x 800
STORAGE: 16GB
PROCESSOR: Dual-core 1.5GHz ARM A9
RAM: 1GB
WEIGHT: 670g
WDH: 273 x 8 x 170mm

noticeably less robust than the Asus Memo Pad FHD 10. The volume and power buttons in particular feel flimsy, and we're not sure we'd feel confident putting the bundled keyboard to extended use. Its tiny keys are too light and lacking in feedback to be comfortable for longer typing sessions. We found it frustratingly fiddly.

A far bigger problem for Archos than the keyboard, though, is the 101 XS's display. The resolution is a bog-standard 800 x 1,280, and quality is well below par. Brightness peaks at only 282cd/m² and, although the contrast is excellent, the fact it's an MVA panel means text and

graphics blur noticeably as you swipe and scroll your way around. Worse still, it has a noticeably grainy look to it.

Performance wasn't very good, either, with below-average scores in our tech tests. Battery life is also unremarkable: it lasted 8hrs 2mins in the looping video test, which is a long way behind the best.

All in all, the 101 XS isn't bad value for money, especially considering the free keyboard cover. It's well connected, too, with a microSD slot and a mini-HDMI output. However, plasticky build and a poor screen mean we'd spend our money elsewhere.

The Fonepad has a good-quality 7in screen with a 800 x 1,280 resolution, and it's joined by a 1.2-megapixel camera.

Asus Fonepad

An absolute bargain of a compact tablet, regardless of whether you're willing to look strange by using the built-in smartphone features in public

The Asus Fonepad is a curious mix of devices. At first glance, it's a standard 7in tablet, but look closer and it also includes 3G and a fully integrated smartphone; it's basically a giant phone handset, so you can go all Dom Joly on the bus home. Gimmick or genius, it certainly stands out.

The chief appeal, aside from being a talking point at the pub, is its great value. It will set you back only £180, and when you think of what you're getting for that money – a smartphone and a 7in 3G tablet similar to the Nexus 7 in one handy package – it's a pretty remarkable buy.

SPECS

PRICE: £180
SCREEN: 7in 800 x 1,280
STORAGE: 16GB
PROCESSOR: Single-core 1.2GHz Intel Atom Z2420
RAM: 1GB
WEIGHT: 316g
WDH: 120 x 11 x 196mm

The physical similarity between the Fonepad and the Nexus 7 is striking, which is not all that surprising given that both are built by Asus. The bezel is the same width, and the screen itself had the same size and 800 x 1,280 resolution as the Nexus 7, until Google released its higher-resolution 2013 update. In the UK, the Fonepad is available with only a front-facing 1.2-megapixel camera – just like the original Nexus 7.

However, there are big differences. Take the rear panel: the Fonepad is made of smooth, matte plastic, while the Nexus 7's was textured and rubbery,

and there's a pop-off panel at the top for access to the tablet's SIM and microSD card slots. The Nexus 7 had no way of expanding storage, but the Fonepad can accommodate another 32GB on top of its internal 16GB.

The other big difference lies inside the Fonepad: you might think its single-core 1.2GHz Intel Atom processor would fall behind the quad-core of the Nexus 7, but benchmark performance is actually comparable. In general use, the Fonepad feels fluid and responsive. Swiping between homescreens and panning and scrolling pages proved a pleasant experience, and it handled all

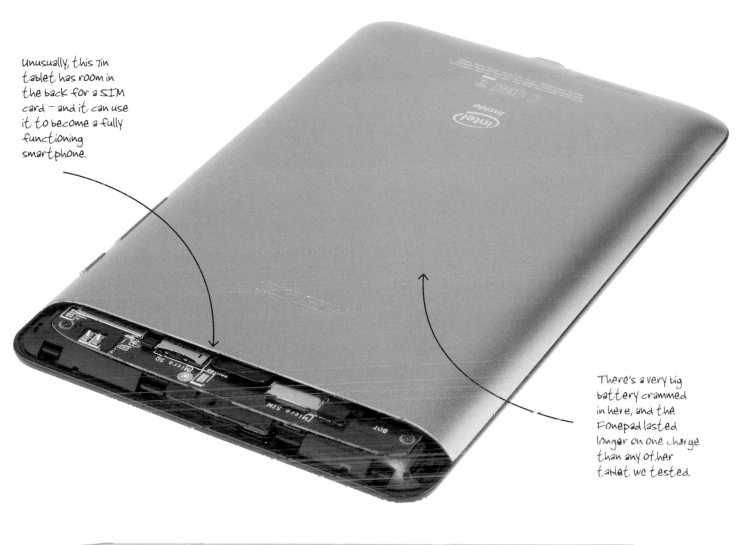

Unusually, this 7in tablet has room in the back for a SIM card – and it can use it to become a fully functioning smartphone.

There's a very big battery crammed in here, and the Fonepad lasted longer on one charge than any other tablet we tested.

Unlike the rubbery Nexus 7, the Fonepad is made of smooth, matte plastic.

the demanding games we threw at it, from Real Racing 3 to Modern Combat 3: Fallen Nation, with few dropped frames.

Plus, it has a very big battery. Curious as to its mobile credentials, we first ran some standard smartphone tests on the Fonepad to see how long it would last, and it proved right up with the very best of today's mobile batteries. And back in our more familiar video-looping tablet test, its result of 12hrs 58mins was the best we've seen from a tablet of its size.

Even the screen quality is good. Its maximum brightness is better than all the compact tablets except the Nexus 7, and colour reproduction is okay, albeit a

touch less vibrant than the best. Our only serious complaint is that the glass picks up greasy fingerprints all too easily, hindering readability outdoors.

The Fonepad is a solid tablet and, technically, a perfectly adequate smartphone, and since it uses a near-stock Android 4.1.2 there's very little wrong with the dialler or contact management side of things, either. But, of course, it has its practical limitations. It's far too wide to be comfortably used in one hand, and the matte rear of the device is slippery, making it difficult to get a secure, one-handed hold on it. Without the usual Gorilla Glass on the

front, it's likely to pick up scratches, too.

Its size also means it simply isn't as practical as a phone to keep on or around you at all times. In the car, you can't place it into any old cubbyhole, and you'll need large pockets if you want to carry it to the shops. Still, a tablet that also doubles up as an occasional phone may appeal, and even if you choose not to make calls the 3G data capability is well worth having.

The Fonepad does have weaknesses, not least the fact that you'll have to wait on Asus for OS updates. But there's no denying the Fonepad packs a hell of a punch for a budget tablet.

The 10in display is a real high point of the Memo Pad FHD 10, and it's well matched by the tablet's strong feature set.

Asus Memo Pad FHD 10

A big, high–quality Full HD screen and a strong design just about outweigh the slightly uneven performance and the limitation regarding games

Asus has made some great tablets of late, with the compact Fonepad and now the Memo Pad range hitting all the right notes. The Memo Pad FHD 10 is exactly what you'd expect: an Android tablet with a 10.1in Full HD IPS display – 1,920 x 1,200 to be precise. For £300, that isn't bad at all.

The quality is decent, too. Although the maximum brightness isn't quite up there with the best, the contrast ratio is good, and that high resolution gives a really crisp, sharp picture.

Compared to similar 10in tablets, the Asus is nice and light, and comfortable to hold for extended periods. We also

SPECS

PRICE: £300
SCREEN: 10.1in 1,920 x 1,200
STORAGE: 16GB
PROCESSOR: Dual-core 1.6GHz Intel Atom Z2560
RAM: 2GB
WEIGHT: 580g
WDH: 265 x 9.5 x 182mm

prefer its soft, dimpled plastic finish to the stickier plastic of Google's devices. A quick glance around the edges reveals a micro-HDMI output and a microSD slot for expanding the tablet's generous 16GB of integrated storage.

It's good so far, but there are flaws. Powering the FHD 10 is a dual-core 1.6GHz Intel Atom processor with 2GB of system RAM, and it runs Android 4.2.2. Navigating even hefty web pages feels smooth, as does the OS in general, but we were perturbed to discover that a degree of typing lag was in evidence. The benchmark results weren't up there with the best, although we did get

smooth gameplay in Real Racing 3. And there's one big red flag: the processor is x86 based, which means it won't be compatible with every app and game on Google Play. The impact will largely depend on your enthusiasm for gaming.

With solid battery life, and a good 5-megapixel rear camera, the Asus Memo Pad FHD 10 looks to be an attractive choice if you like your tablets big. It has plenty of storage and a slot to add more; it has a solid, all-round design and its performance is good enough, if not stellar. Whether all that's enough to overlook the many excellent, smaller devices will depend on your budget.

Tablet cases

Although you won't get the wide range of choice enjoyed by iPad users, the most popular Android devices do have custom cases – you just need to shop around

Asus Travel Cover for Nexus 7
Price: £20 Supplier: www.johnlewis.com

The new Google Nexus 7 has one of the biggest ranges of available accessories, so be sure to browse before buying. This straightforward protective case is made by Asus – the tablet's manufacturer – so you can be certain it will fit the Nexus 7's dimensions snugly and offer a good level of protection on the move.

Tuff-Luv Slim-Stand Faux Leather Case
Price: £30 Supplier: www.tuff-luv.com

With the might of Amazon behind it, it's no surprise that the Kindle Fire HD has a decent amount of accessories from a wide range of companies. This faux leather cover for the 8.9in model has three grooves for positioning the tablet at different angles, and it automatically puts your tablet to sleep when you close the case.

Samsung Galaxy Note 8.0 Book Cover
Price: £38 Supplier: www.mobile-fun.co.uk

For a tablet that's meant to be used in portrait orientation like a book, it makes perfect sense to buy a book-style cover. This official case clips to the back of the Galaxy Note 8, with a folding cover on the front; to prop the device up, flip the cover round the back into one of two different angles. Ideal for switching from note taking to movie watching.

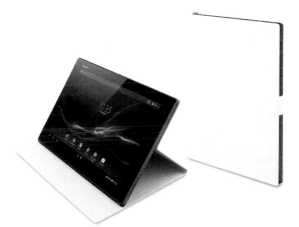

Roxfit Sony Xperia Tablet Z Case
Price: £17 Supplier: www.mobile-fun.co.uk

Officially licensed for the Sony Xperia Tablet Z, this ultraslim case is like many others in that it converts from a neat book-style carrying case into a folding stand for using the tablet on a flat surface. It fits perfectly, leaving access to all ports and buttons, and comes with a secure magnetic latch to keep everything in place.

Accessories

From Bluetooth keyboards to portable charging stations, there are plenty of accessories you can buy to enhance your Android tablet

Freedom i-Connex
Price: £30   Supplier: www.mobilefun.co.uk

This folding keyboard has large, near-desktop-sized keys, despite its small size. We found it easy to get up to top speed. Embedded in one half is a pull-out, folding smartphone stand; there are media keys down the left edge; and rubber feet keep it in place. It remembers four pairings, so you can easily switch from device to device. A tempting choice.

Triggertrap
Price: £25 cable; Free app   Supplier: www.amazon.co.uk

Triggertrap is a smartphone or tablet remote release system for photographers. Just download the app onto your tablet, connect the dongle and camera cable together, then plug one end into the tablet's headphone connector and the other into the camera's release socket. It has all manner of great shooting options.

Mophie Juice Pack Powerstation Duo
Price: £81   Supplier: www.ebuyer.com

Although it's advertised as for the iPad, this device's two USB outputs mean it can charge any Android tablet as well – and even handle two at once. This 196g device contains a 6,000mAh battery, which can charge a tablet several times before it itself needs a recharge. It isn't cheap, but it can be a lifesaver on the road.

TYLT PowerPlant
Price: £60   Supplier: www.tylt.com

Designed to hold charge for a year, the aptly named PowerPlant can fully recharge most compact Android tablets. Measuring 78 x 44 x 33mm – think a credit card on steroids – it takes up barely any space in a bag, and it features a built-in micro-USB cable, too. There's even a USB port for charging a second device simultaneously.

Griffin Stylus for Capacitive Touchscreens
Price: £10 Supplier: www.amazon.co.uk

If you like the idea of using a pen to prod your tablet, you don't have to buy one that comes with the feature included. You can buy a third-party stylus such as this basic one from Griffin, and use its soft nib in place of your finger. For a little more money, you can get a version that doubles up as a normal pen and even a laser pointer.

AmazonBasics Portable Travel Stand
Price: £8 Supplier: www.amazon.co.uk

If you want to go really cheap and cheerful, Amazon makes its own very simple stand, ostensibly for the Kindle Fire HD devices but it should fit all but the biggest of Android tablets. It offers good support in use, and folds up nice and small when you're done with it, making it an ideal travelling companion.

Kensington Chaise Universal Tablet Stand
Price: £12 Supplier: www.kensington.com

You don't need to buy a stand that's specific to your tablet; many universal stands will fit all kind of shapes and sizes. The Chaise Universal Tablet Stand is an exceedingly simple piece of kit, which flips open to a range of angles to hold your tablet steady in the tightest of spots. It's very well priced, too.

Griffin Beacon for Android
Price: £50 Supplier: www.amazon.co.uk

The Griffin Beacon is a portable wireless transmitter for Android tablets, which allows you to use your tablet as a remote control for a variety of TV and audio equipment. You pair it with the free Dijit app, which has a built-in library of thousands of common devices, so setup and operation are simple.

HARDWARE REVIEWS

The Nexus 7's stunning screen has a resolution of 1,200 x 1,920 – the highest we've ever seen on a compact tablet.

Google Nexus 7

An extraordinary compact tablet that improves on the original Nexus 7 in almost every way, once again showing rivals how it's done

The original Nexus 7 blew the compact tablet competition away when it first launched in 2012, so we were very keen to see how Google would update it. Now it's here, we're delighted to say the 2013 update takes that superb template and improves on it in multiple ways.

It might look a bit taller and thinner than the old model, but the height and screen size actually haven't changed; the reason for the new skinnier look is that the hardware manufacturer Asus has slimmed down the side bezels by 6mm, making the new model just 114mm wide.

SPECS

PRICE: £199
SCREEN: 7in 1,200 x 1,920
STORAGE: 16GB
PROCESSOR: Quad-core 1.5GHz Snapdragon S4 Pro
RAM: 2GB
WEIGHT: 290g
WDH: 114 x 8.5 x 200mm

This has the slightly unfortunate effect of making the top and bottom bezels feel even bigger than they did before – an effect that's exacerbated by Android's black notification and button bars at the top and bottom of the screen. Still, you quickly become accustomed to the long shape, and it's hard to complain about getting the same amount of screen in a slightly smaller overall package.

The new Nexus 7 is also lighter than before, down from 340g to 290g – a palpable 15% reduction in mass over the previous generation – and thinner, too, measuring only 8.5mm thick. That

isn't quite as slim as an iPad mini, but it's the thinnest and lightest Android tablet we've seen. Don't confuse thin with flimsy, however: there's very little flex to the back of it, and with scratch-resistant Corning glass covering the front we'd have no qualms about tossing this tablet into a bag.

There's good stuff on the inside, too. The 1.5GHz quad-core Snapdragon S4 Pro is a beast of a processor that really ups the performance from last year's model – and it's supported by an unusually generous 2GB of RAM, plus a fast GPU. This being a Google product, it comes with the very latest Android 4.3

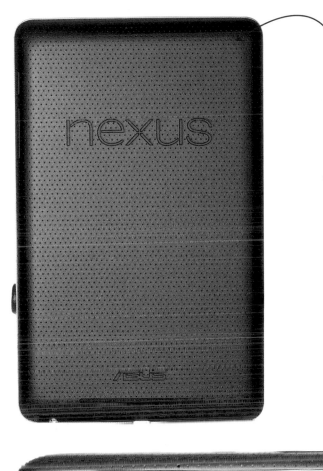

The new Nexus 7 has a 5-megapixel camera on the rear, for snapping high-quality photos on the move.

It's the thinnest and lightest compact tablet available today.

It may be a very slim tablet, but there's a very good battery crammed inside.

Images from the rear camera are a little cold and noisy, but the quality is fine for snapshots. You also get support for Bluetooth 4, "SlimPort" HDMI (although compatible adaptors aren't yet widely available) and Qi wireless charging, plus, as before, GPS, NFC and the latest dual-band 802.11n Wi-Fi.

With all this great hardware stuffed into such a slim case, you might expect the power consumption to be a weak point. The 3,950mAh rating of the internal battery is indeed below average, yet impressively the device lasted 11hrs 48mins in our standard battery tests. That's 1hr 10mins short of the Asus Fonepad, but well ahead of most other compacts; for comparison, the original 2012 Nexus 7 managed only 8hrs 48mins.

If you really want to find niggles with the Nexus 7, you can. For a start, there's no microSD card slot to expand on the base 16GB of storage should the need arise. The speakers aren't very loud, and their low end response is distinctly lacking. The power and volume buttons at the right-hand side are set almost flush with the case, making them awkward to press.

Plus, although the original Nexus 7 seemed like incredible value at the time of its release, this new model must be evaluated against some very cheap additions to the compact tablet line-up.

What you get for that Nexus premium, however, is a superlative piece of hardware. Put simply, it's the fastest, lightest, thinnest and narrowest compact Android tablet available, with the crispest Full HD screen as well. And, because it's a Nexus, you know the Android OS will be well supported for the foreseeable future and won't get bogged down by any third-party "enhancements".

If you just want a cheap and capable tablet, there are perfectly usable alternatives out there. But if you're in the market for something more elegant, more capable and more future-proof, for only a little more money, the 2013 Google Nexus 7 is more or less irresistible.

OS, and those powerful internals make flicking around the interface a wonderfully snappy experience.

The full power of the hardware really shone through in our benchmarks, where it was anywhere between 30% and 65% faster than the old Nexus 7. That performance is even more impressive when you take into account the number of pixels it's processing. A fantastic new 1,200 x 1,920 IPS display represents the highest resolution we've seen on a compact tablet, delivering a pixel density way higher than Apple's Retina iPads. As you'd expect, this makes black-on-white text and

vector-based apps such as Maps look absolutely pristine. Video content and games look bold and bright, too, helped by a searing maximum brightness and very high contrast. Colours on our test model verged slightly towards the cool side, but not by enough to suck the warmth out of the picture. In fact, our only real problem was that a screen this sharp tends to expose the weaknesses of the countless low-resolution images you'll find online.

On top of this, the new Nexus 7 has a 5-megapixel rear-facing autofocus camera, to partner the fixed-focus 1.2-megapixel camera on the front.

The Slate 7 comes with HP's Beats Audio technology and two cameras, so it's quite feature-packed for the price.

HP Slate 7

HP has crafted a solid, attractive tablet for a superb price, but the Slate 7 simply cuts too many corners to earn a recommendation

HP's little 7in tablet packs a lot in, with front- and rear-facing cameras, a microSD slot and HP's proprietary Beats Audio for a remarkable price of £100. Despite that, physically the Slate 7 looks and feels like a premium piece of kit. At 370g, it's not the lightest, but despite a little flex in the plastic rear the solid chassis feels built to last.

Alas, the all-important 7in screen betrays HP's stretched budget. Its 600 x 1,024 resolution is far less crisp than its rivals, and it feels narrow and cramped in use. The maximum brightness is adequate, but the poor black level

SPECS

PRICE: £100
SCREEN: 7in 600 x 1,024
STORAGE: 8GB
PROCESSOR: Dual-core 1.6GHz ARM A9
RAM: 1GB
WEIGHT: 370g
WDH: 116 x 11 x 197mm

washes out the picture. Colours are subdued, and a graininess leaves blocks of colour looking dirty and mottled.

With a dual-core 1.6GHz ARM A9 processor and 1GB of RAM, we hoped performance would be better, but whether flicking between homescreens or scrolling and zooming web pages, things were noticeably juddery. Benchmarks were also hit and miss, and despite the chunky feel of the chassis its relatively small 3,500mAh battery lasted just 6hrs 37mins in our video test.

As for features, HP has had to perform something of a juggling act to squeeze in its highlights. There's only

8GB of onboard storage, although it does have a microSD expansion slot. HP has also opted to stick with single-band 802.11n Wi-Fi and Bluetooth 2.1 to keep costs down. It has both 0.3-megapixel front and 3-megapixel rear cameras, but neither works well. The front camera captures smeary, heavily compressed, low-resolution images, and the rear camera struggles to produce decent snaps even in good light, with photos dogged by noise and lacking in detail.

We like the attractive hardware and the low price, but HP has had to cut too many corners to hit it. You can get much better for only a bit more money.

The IdeaTab S6000 only costs £200, yet it comes with a big 10in screen.

Lenovo IdeaTab S6000

As a big 10in tablet for only £200, you could argue it's a good-value choice, but it does absolutely nothing in design or performance to stand out

Lenovo has made some exotic hybrid devices recently, but the IdeaTab S6000 is a much more sensible device. It's a straight Android 4.2 10.1in tablet, clad in a rather creaky, dark grey textured plastic, with no sign of fancier materials. That large display has only a 1,280 x 800 resolution, you get a standard 16GB of integrated storage, and connectivity is perfunctory, with only single-band 802.11n Wi-Fi, no NFC and no full-sized USB ports.

There are a couple of bright spots in the specification, with Micro-HDMI for outputting the picture to a TV, and a microSD slot for expanding the storage.

SPECS

PRICE: £200
SCREEN: 10.1in 1,280 x 800
STORAGE: 16GB
PROCESSOR: Quad-core 1.2GHz MediaTek
RAM: 1GB
WEIGHT: 562g
WDH: 259 x 9 x 180mm

And, for a budget £200 device, Lenovo's kept things surprisingly slim and light, measuring 9mm thick and weighing a reasonable 562g. Battery life is decent, too, with the IdeaTab S6000 lasting 10hrs 39mins in our looping video test.

On balance, then, we like the hardware, but performance is disappointing. The quad-core 1.2GHz MediaTek processor clearly isn't up to the rigours of the latest intensive 3D games: Real Racing 3 and the power-hungry Minion Rush felt choppy. We also experienced typing lag when using the stock Android keyboard, which is never a good sign for a modern tablet,

although scrolling, panning and zooming web pages was smooth enough. Perhaps more of a problem, though, is the quality of the screen, which in our tests proved worryingly dim, even at maximum brightness. It's rather grainy, too, which doesn't help.

Overall, the Lenovo IdeaTab S6000 isn't bad value for that £200. It's slim and light for its screen size, its battery life is decent, and we reckon we could live with the slightly sluggish performance and dim screen in daily use. There are better choices out there, but you could do a lot worse if you want a big tablet for a small price.

ESSENTIAL APPS *for advanced users*

If you want to take control of your Android tablet, there's a host of advanced apps on Google Play that allow you to do it – here's our pick of the best

Tasker
Price: £1.85

Tablets are complicated beasts, and keeping on top of all their settings can sometimes feel like a full-time job. Tasker is an automation app that aims to take the sting out of toggling your options and allows you to create various commands and rules to make things run more smoothly. For example, you can create a task that dims the tablet's screen and switches off wireless connections when the battery drops to a certain level, or have an app start up the moment you plug in some headphones. Tasker is a power user's download but, once mastered, it will become one of your favourite companions.

Titanium Backup
Price: Free

To use Titanium Backup you'll need a rooted device, which means looking at the tablet's firmware to gain admin rights. Thereafter, you'll be able to back up all your apps and data, allowing far greater control over your content. For example, you save game information or configuration settings, even if you lose your tablet or upgrade to a new one. A Pro version offers the chance to "freeze" applications to prevent them from soaking up system memory, making your tablet even faster than usual.

Screebl
Price: £1.23

There are few things more annoying than your tablet screen constantly switching off when you're using it. Thankfully, there's a solution: Screebl uses your device's motion sensors to detect when it's being used, and prevents your screen from going into sleep mode. It also helps save battery, as it shuts off the display when it senses the tablet being laid down on a flat surface. It's surprisingly effective – use it once and you'll never want to be without it again.

ROM Manager

Price: Free

This is another app that requires root admin access, but is absolutely essential if you're looking to enter the wild and often scary world of ROM flashing. ROMs are basically new skins for your tablet: they can add new features and functionality or radically change the way your tablet works. Unless you're using a Nexus device, this is usually the best way of keeping your tablet up to date with the latest features offered by Android. ROM Manager also allows you to back up your current ROM and get "over the air" updates for your new one. Just be aware that it needs to be used with caution.

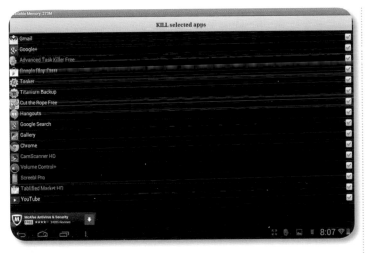

Advanced Task Killer
Price: Free

Android's multitasking capability means you can jump between apps without having to shut them down, but there's an obvious drawback: having too many apps running at once can seriously slow down your device. Advanced Task Killer allows you to kill all apps in a single click, or set auto-kill on certain unwanted processes. It needs to be used with care – killing all apps can sometimes make your tablet unstable – but it's a powerful tool.

Advanced Touchpad
Price: Free

If you have a PC in your living room that you use as a media playback device, you may be looking for a more elegant way to control it than a wired keyboard and mouse. Advanced Touchpad turns your humble tablet into a remote for your computer, connecting to it via your Wi-Fi network, allowing you to operate the system effortlessly. That means less junk taking up valuable space in your living room. You can use Advanced Touchpad with your desktop PC, as well.

The 5-megapixle rear camera also shoots 720p video, and there's a microSD slot in case you need to expand the 16GB of storage.

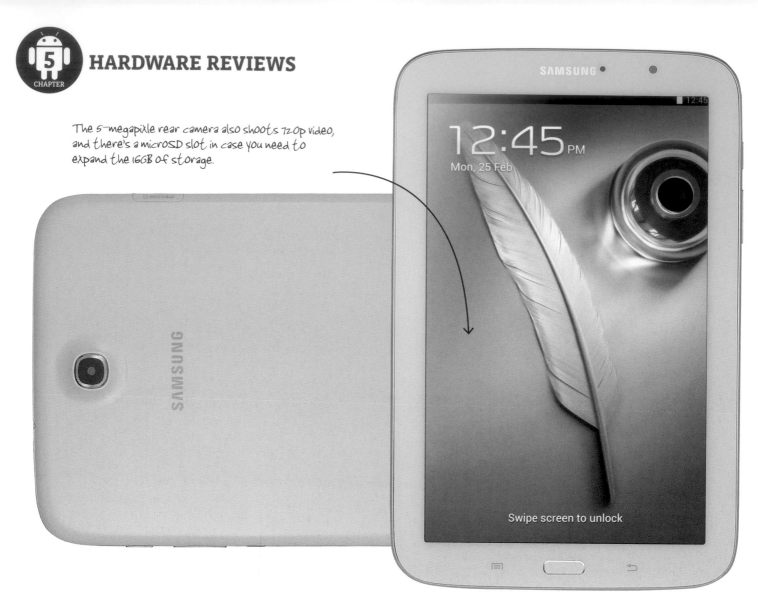

Samsung Galaxy Note 8.0

It's one of the best compact tablets on the market, with innovative stylus capabilities, but it comes with a disappointingly hefty price tag

The major compact tablet manufacturers all seem to see the future in different screen sizes, and it's clear that Samsung is a big fan of 8in as the sweet spot. The Galaxy Note 8.0 has a lot of competition, though, so we were keen to see how one of the biggest names in consumer electronics would make a product that really stands out.

Samsung's answer is pen input. The Galaxy Note 8.0 comes with a Wacom-based S Pen stylus, which stows neatly into a slot in the bottom-right corner of the tablet. It's pressure sensitive and far more accurate than a capacitive stylus,

SPECS

PRICE: £340
SCREEN: 8in 800 x 1,280
STORAGE: 16GB
PROCESSOR: Quad-core 1.6GHz Exynos 4412
RAM: 2GB
WEIGHT: 340g
WDH: 136 x 8 x 211mm

making the Note 8.0 ideal for note taking, creative sketching or fine photo-editing tasks. It's even possible to enter text via handwriting recognition, using a panel built into the stock Samsung keyboard, and it's something that works surprisingly well. In fact, where the S Pen feels a little gimmicky on a smaller device such as the Galaxy Note II, it's far more practical here, where the larger screen makes for a more comfortable experience.

Another unusual feature is the ability to use the 3G model as a giant phone, much like the Asus Fonepad. Alas, we haven't been able to test this as

Samsung only sent us the Wi-Fi model, although at only £40 or so more it isn't that much to spend on top of the standard version. Again, though, you'll look rather odd holding this 8in device up to your ear in public.

Physically, the Samsung Galaxy Note 8.0 treads familiar ground. The rear panel is constructed of glossy plastic, just like on Samsung's flagship smartphones over the past couple of years; the trim is silver plastic, and the glass front is smooth under the finger. The whole shebang weighs 340g and, although it flexes a fair bit when twisted, it does feel well put together.

The Galaxy Note 8.0 has a great screen, and it's made even better by the inclusion of a stylus for note taking.

The stylus slots neatly into a hole in the bottom corner of the tablet, ready to be pulled out when precision is required.

In terms of size, it's taller, wider and thicker than an iPad mini, but we're not talking huge differences. In fact, the broader screen surround makes the Galaxy Note 8.0 the more comfortable device to hold one-handed.

As with Samsung's smartphones, there's plenty of practicality on show. There's a microSD slot for expanding the device's 16GB of onboard storage; the micro-USB socket on the bottom edge is used for charging the device as well as data transfer; and the tablet is stuffed with bundled software, covering everything from music streaming to photo editing.

The Galaxy Note 8.0 runs Samsung's TouchWiz overlay on top of Android 4.1, and this is packed with tools and features, although at first it does feel a little overwhelming.

As this is a premium product, it's no surprise to find it has both front- and rear-facing cameras, although there's no LED flash to help out in low light. The snapper on the rear is a 5-megapixel unit that shoots 720p video, and the one on the front captures 1.3-megapixel images. Quality from the rear camera is surprisingly good, with crisp, well-balanced images produced in good light. Low-light performance is much less impressive, though, with photos becoming soft, blurry and lacking in contrast.

The screen is a high point. Although the resolution is a mere 800 x 1,280 – rather left behind by the Full HD panel of the Nexus 7 – the image quality is superlative. It has a ridiculously high maximum brightness that's far better than an iPad mini, and the colours it produces are beautifully vivid.

Performance is excellent, too. It smashed many rivals in our intensive benchmarks, and in real-world use the Galaxy Note 8.0's 1.6GHz quad-core Exynos processor and fast graphics chip are clearly up to the job, with smooth frame rates in all the games we threw at it. All this power does take its toll on battery life, though. In our looping video test, it lasted 7hrs 44mins, which is about acceptable for its size, but well short of the best compact tablets on the market.

All in all, the Samsung Galaxy Note 8.0 is a superb compact tablet with some unique features that set it apart from the competition. Its screen, camera and performance are all superb, and the stylus capability is genuinely useful and usable.

However, there is one big problem, and that's the price. At £340, it's a lot more expensive than Apple's iPad mini, and pricier even than many 10in Android tablets. Unless that pen will really make a difference to your daily routine, the Galaxy Note 8.0 will be a tough sell.

You won't find many better screens than this 10in panel, with a Full HD resolution and superb colours.

Sony Xperia Tablet Z

A superbly accomplished Android tablet with some unique features – water resistance and an infrared transmitter stand out – and only one real weakness: the price

For a long time in 2013, it seemed that no manufacturer really fancied its chances against the might of Apple and Google in the 10in tablet market. Until, that is, eventually Sony arrived with a new challenger.

The Xperia Tablet Z is typical Sony – stylish and built to a very high standard – and we're extremely glad it's here, because we now have one heck of a good Android tablet to put up against the big guns.

The thing you notice upon picking up the Xperia Tablet Z for the very first time is just how light and slim it is. Even the latest iPad feels lumpen next to this

SPECS

PRICE: From £399
SCREEN: 10.1in 1,920 x 1,080
STORAGE: 16GB
PROCESSOR: Quad-core 1.5GHZ Snapdragon S4 Pro
RAM: 2GB
WEIGHT: 467g
WDH: 266 x 6.9 x 172mm

lightweight marvel, and yet it's no insubstantial waif. Give it a twist and, yes, it does give a little, but there's no creaking or crunching in doing so.

It also has a nice surprise to spring: water and dust resistance. Every port around the edges of the Tablet Z comes with a flap to seal it shut, giving it an everyday robustness that can't be matched by any other tablet on the market (aside from more expensive specialist business equipment). This is the kind of tablet you can take along for entertainment on a summer camping holiday without worrying about the dangers of damp.

This being Sony, it's also a tablet that's completely at home on the sofa. An infrared transmitter set into the top edge of the Xperia Tablet Z allows it to be used as a glorified universal remote control and, since this capability is baked right into the OS, you can pop up the remote app at any time simply by tapping an icon in the button bar at the bottom of the screen.

On the subject of displays, the Tablet Z's 1,920 x 1,080 panel is typically excellent. Even against tablets with a slightly higher 1,920 x 1,200 resolution, you have to look very closely to make out any extra grain on the Sony's

The Sony's party trick is water and dust resistance, making it more durable than most tablets.

picture. The screen performed well in our tests, with beautifully saturated, vivid colours coming at the slight expense of some highlight and shadow detail. The brightness and contrast are both good, too.

It's all good so far, but the Tablet Z's real strength is its performance. Under the hood is a potent quad-core 1.5GHz Snapdragon S4 Pro processor, which delivered flawless responsiveness in and around the operating system at all times. Apps fired up quickly and with no delay; we found no typing lag, even though the default keyboard is a proprietary Sony one; and manipulating

An infrared transmitter in the top edge lets you use the Xperia Tablet Z as your TV remote control.

web pages was always silky smooth.

In our performance benchmarks, it again impressed, outdoing all the other Android tablets we've tested in some of our graphics tests. Games ran smoothly, so you can throw all the latest titles at the Tablet Z without a worry.

And this power thankfully doesn't come at the expense of battery life. The Tablet Z gave us an excellent 12hrs 26mins of looping video, right up there with the best around. Only the camera disappoints, with heavy handed compression spoiling its ability to pick up fine details, despite a high 8.1-megapixel sensor.

Overall, the Sony Tablet Z is an excellent addition to the ranks of larger Android tablets. It's quick and responsive in all kinds of use, light and slim with the added bonus of water and dust resistance, plus it comes with an infrared transmitter, expandable memory and excellent battery life. It's a very strong feature list.

You might get better value for money elsewhere, as Sony devices are always at the high end of the scale, but if you're after the most accomplished Android tablet around and don't mind paying a premium, you won't be disappointed.

ANDROID FOR TABLETS
GLOSSARY

3G/4G The type of data connection first used by all smartphones, laptops and tablets, 3G allows you to connect to the internet wherever you can get a good mobile phone signal. You revert to the slower HSDPA in the absence of a 3G signal. Newer devices are beginning to adopt the faster 4G technology, although it may not be widely available outside of major cities while the networks expand their coverage, and as with all new technologies you tend to pay more for the faster data speeds.

720p/1080p See HD video.

A

Adobe Flash Player See Flash.

B

Bluetooth A wireless technology used for the connection of peripheral devices such as keyboards, mice and headsets, and also for tethering your tablet to a mobile phone to use its data connection. Typically has a close range of 10 metres or less.

C

Capacitive (touchscreen) Used in most of today's tablets and smartphones, capacitive touchscreens require a much gentler touch to activate than resistive types. They can sometimes even sense a finger a few millimetres above the surface.

cd/m² This is the measurement of screen brightness. It stands for candela per metre squared, and we measure it using a piece of equipment called a colorimeter. The maximum figure is derived from a white screen with the tablet's brightness setting at maximum.

F

Flash A special type of web technology that allows website developers to place more advanced and interactive elements on pages, such as video players and games. The iPad famously doesn't support Flash, but until recently most modern Android tablets did support it. Support has been dropped from the most recent version of Android's Chrome browser. Many sites built using Flash are switching to the more widely compatible HTML5.

fps Movies are made up of many thousands of still images played in sequence to give the impression of smooth movement. Frames per second, or fps, is essentially a measurement of that sequence and indicates the frequency with which a video camera captures a scene – the higher the fps, the smoother the video.

Froyo Google's codename for Android 2.2. As an out-of-date version, it's only used on low-cost smartphones and tablets today.

G

Gingerbread Google's codename for Android 2.3. Again, commonly only used on budget smartphones and tablets.

GPS Standing for Global Positioning System, the GPS "radio" chip enables devices to pinpoint their geographical position and so provide location-based services. GPS requires a view of the sky to receive a signal from GPS satellites, so doesn't work indoors, although tablets can still establish a loose position by analysing local Wi-Fi hotspots and matching them against Google's database.

H

HD video There are two types of HD video – 720p and 1080p (or Full HD) – and the difference between the two is essentially the number of pixels used (the resolution). A 720p HD video is 1,280 pixels wide and 720 pixels high; a 1080p HD video is 1,920 x 1,080 pixels. The more pixels in a video picture, the more detail can be displayed.

HDMI A type of digital video connection that allows devices to be connected directly to an HDTV or modern monitor. Tablets typically use either mini- or micro-HDMI ports, but cables are rarely included.

Honeycomb Google's codename for Android version 3, which was a breakthrough at the time as it was the first version designed specifically for tablets.

HSDPA See 3G.

I

Ice Cream Sandwich The codename for Android version 4, Ice Cream Sandwich finally unified the smartphone and tablet operating systems, giving both types of device a similar look and feel. It's the minimum you should look for in a purchase if you want a modern tablet experience.

IPS Stands for "in-plane switching", a type of TFT screen technology used in more expensive monitors and tablets, become becoming more and more common. IPS displays boast superior colours and wider viewing angles to standard TFT screens.

J

Jelly Bean The codename for Android version 4.1, Jelly Bean introduced new features and greatly improved tablet performance. Also saw the debut of the Google Now locational service.

K

KitKat

The codename for the upcoming Android version 4.4, due out on devices in late 2013. Google has partnered with Nestle for this version, so expect to see much cross-promotion between the two brands.

M

Megapixels

Refers to the total number of pixels a tablet's camera is able to resolve. A camera that shoots 5-megapixel stills (five million total pixels) produces images with a resolution of 2,592 x 1,944. Much like HD video, more pixels generally means a better-quality image

microSD

Like the SD cards used in digital cameras, but much smaller, microSD cards allow you to expand the integrated storage of your tablet on the cheap so you can fit in more music, video and other files. The latest devices accept 64GB cards, with many limited to 32GB. If you're buying a tablet without much internal storage, make sure it has one of these slots.

Multitouch

Refers to the ability of a touchscreen to accept input from more than one point on a screen simultaneously. Multitouch screens allow the use of advanced gestures, such as the pinching in and out of the fingers to zoom in and out of web pages, and the rotation of photos with two fingers. Multitouch also allows more effective keyboard data entry, as you can hold down Shift to type capital letters. On today's modern tablets, multitouch screens are included as standard.

Resistive (touchscreen)

This is the cheapest type of touchscreen technology available to manufacturers, and one that is becoming less and less common. A resistive touchscreen requires pressure on the screen to activate buttons and links. They're generally to be avoided, as they (usually) don't support multitouch and aren't particularly responsive or accurate. You'll generally only find them on the very cheapest tablets.

P

Panorama

The Android camera app can now take panoramic photos, where you pan your camera from left to right across a scene and the software compiles one long image.

Photo sphere

Much like the panorama (see above), a photo sphere is a collection of photos taken all around a scene, automatically compiled into a single picture.

S

Stop motion

Like Nick Park's Wallace and Gromit animations, stop-motion refers to a movie created from many thousands of snapped still images, which skilled animators then bring to life. Android 4 tablets have a stop-motion tool built into the video camera app, which snaps still images at predefined intervals then stitches them all together for you.

Streaming

Refers to the process of playing video or music files stored in a remote location on your tablet, without physically copying the file to its local storage. Good examples of this are BBC iPlayer and YouTube videos, where a website stores the file and streams it via a special web page-based video player. You can also play media files hosted on a networked PC or Mac using a client/server app such as Plex.

Stylus

A pen-like input device for writing directly onto a tablet screen.

T

Tethering

If your tablet doesn't have a 3G chip, you can "tether" it to your smartphone to piggyback on its internet connection. Watch out, though, as you'll be racking up data on your mobile phone contract, which may have its own monthly data cap.

TFT

This is the standard type of screen used in tablets today. TFT stands for "thin-film transistor", but due to variations in manufacture, quality control and the electronics behind them, there's a vast difference in quality between different tablets.

U

USB

There are several different types of USB connection, but all allow the connection of two devices together for the purposes of transferring files. Android tablets can usually be connected to a PC or Mac using a micro- or mini-USB socket. Some have a full-sized USB socket, which allows the connection of USB memory sticks and hard disk drives, keyboards and mice.

V

Viewing angles

Not all tablet screens are made equal, and poor viewing angles can seriously affect your enjoyment. With a tablet that has narrow viewing angles, the screen must be held square onto the eye line. As soon as it's tilted slightly away, the colours shift, making viewing difficult.

W

Wi-Fi

The wireless technology included in all of today's devices, Wi-Fi lets you hook into a broadband connection at home (or at a hotel/café-based hotspot) to get online. There are several types of Wi-Fi, denominated by cryptic phraseology and acronyms in the tablet's specifications: 802.11g is the older, slower type; 802.11n is more modern, faster and may also allow a tablet to connect from further away. Look out for tablets with dual-band Wi-Fi; these can connect to modern routers on a newer, less congested Wi-Fi band that often gets faster speeds and less interference.

ANDROID FOR TABLETS
CREDITS

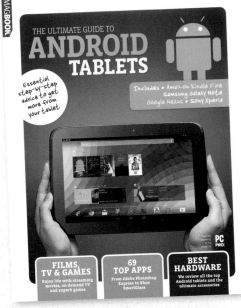

EDITORIAL
Editor Jonathan Bray: jonb@pcpro.co.uk
Managing Editor Priti Patel
Production Editor Rachel Storry
Design & Layout Jo Clements, Sarah Ratcliffe, Heather Reeves
Contributors David Bayon, Damien McFerran

LICENSING & SYNDICATION
Licensing Carlotta Serantoni
carlotta_serantoni@dennis.co.uk, +44 20 7907 6550
Syndication Anj Dosaj-Halai
anj_dosaj-halai@dennis.co.uk, +44 20 7907 6132

ADVERTISING & MARKETING
MagBook Account Manager Katie Wood +44 20 7907 6689
Production Manager Nicky Baker +44 20 7907 6056
MagBook Manager Dharmesh Mistry +44 20 7907 6100

MANAGEMENT
Managing Director John Garewal +44 20 7907 6000
Deputy Managing Director Tim Danton
MD of Advertising Julian Lloyd-Evans
Newstrade Director David Barker
MD of Enterprise Martin Belson
Chief Operating Officer Brett Reynolds
Group Finance Director Ian Leggett
Chief Executive James Tye
Chairman Felix Dennis

The "MagBook" brand is a trademark of Dennis Publishing Ltd, 30 Cleveland St, London W1T 4JD. Company registered in England. All material © Dennis Publishing Ltd, licensed by Felden 2013, and may not be reproduced in whole or part without the consent of the publishers.

LIABILITY

PRINTED BY

Polestar, Bicester, Oxfordshire.

The paper used within this MagBook is produced from sustainable fibre, manufactured by mills with a valid chain of custody.

ISBN 1-78106-172-6